RUSSI[A]
REVOLUTIO[N]
COUNTER-REVOLUTION
1917–1924

John Daborn
Head of History
Dinnington Comprehensive School,
South Yorkshire

CAMBRIDGE
UNIVERSITY PRESS

PUBLISHED BY THE PRESS SYNDICATE OF THE UNIVERSITY OF CAMBRIDGE
The Pitt Building, Trumpington Street, Cambridge, United Kingdom

CAMBRIDGE UNIVERSITY PRESS
The Edinburgh Building, Cambridge CB2 2RU, UK   http://www.cup.cam.ac.uk
40 West 20th Street, New York, NY 10011–4211, USA   http://www.cup.org
10 Stamford Road, Oakleigh, Melbourne 3166, Australia

First published 1991
Fifth printing 1999

Printed in the United Kingdom at the University Press, Cambridge

A catalogue record for this book is available from the British Library

Library of Congress Cataloguing in Publication data
Daborn, John.
  Russia: Revolution and Counter-revolution. 1917–1924 / John Daborn.
  p.   cm.
  Bibliography: p.
  Includes index.
  ISBN 0-521-36790-5
  1. Soviet Union – History – Revolution. 1917–1924.   2. Soviet Union – History – Revolution.
1917–1924 – Economic aspects.   I. Title.
  DK265.D23   1990   89-36124
  947.084′1 – cc20   CIP

ISBN 0 521 36790 5

US

Acknowledgements

The author and publisher are grateful to the following for permission to reproduce extracts and illustrations:

Extracts   1.1, 2.14, 3.9 L. Trotsky, *The History of the Russian Revolution*, Pluto Press, London, 1932, 1977, 1980; 1.2, 1.3, 1.6, 1.8, 1.10, 1.12, 2.4, 2.6, 2.7, 2.13 F. A. Golder, *Documents of Russian History*, Peter Smith Publisher Inc., 1964, Gloucester, MA; 1.4 Alexander Shlyapnikov, *On the Eve of 1917*, Allison & Busby Ltd, 1982; 1.13, 3.1, 3.3(a), 3.7 N. N. Sukhanov, *The Russian Revolution 1917. A Personal Memoir*, edited and translated by Joel Carmichael; 5.10(a), 5.10(b), 6.5(b), 7.6(a), 7.6(b), 7.7(b) V. Serge, *Memoirs of a Revolutionary*, translated and edited by Peter Sedgwick, 1963, Oxford University Press, 1955; 1.14, 2.10 M. McCauley, *The Russian Revolution and the Soviet State 1917–21*, 1975, 4.4(b), 4.4(c), 4.4(e), 4.4(f) N. Harding, *Lenin's Political Thought*, 1983, 5.4(a) J. W. Wheeler-Bennett, *Brest-Litovsk: The Forgotten Peace March 1918*, 1966; 7.12 E. H. Carr, *The Interregnum 1923–4*, MacMillan Publishers Ltd; 2.5, 3.4, 4.2, 4.4(a), 4.4(d), 4.4(g) V. I. Lenin, *Selected Works*, 1977 edition; 3.2, 3.3(b), 4.8(a), 6.2, 6.7, 6.9, 7.3, 7.4, 7.8, 7.10, 7.11 V. I. Lenin, *Collected Works*, 4.3, 4.7, 4.9, 5.1, 5.5, 6.1 Y. Akhapkin. *First Decrees of Soviet Power*, 1970, reprinted by permission of Lawrence & Wishart Ltd; 2.8 cited in Marc Ferro, *The Bolshevik Revolution – A Social History of the Russian Revolution*, Georges Borchardt, Inc., 1985; 3.8 P. A. Milyukov, *History of the Second Russian Revolution*, Holt, Rinehart & Winston, 1959; 4.5(b), 4.8(b), 4.8(c), 5.8, 6.4(a), 6.4(b), 6.5(a), 6.8(a), 6.10(a), 6.10(b) reprinted from *The Bolshevik Revolution, 1917–1918* by James Bunyan and H. H. Fisher with the permission of the publishers, Stanford University Press. © 1934 by the Board of Trustees of the Leland Stanford Junior University; 4.10 Louis de Robien, *Journal diun diplomate*, Albin Michel, 1967; 4.11(a), 4.11(b) E. H. Carr, *The Bolshevik Revolution*, Curtis Brown, London, 1973; 5.2(b) G. Hosking, *A History of the Soviet Union*, 1985, Collins and Harvard University Press; 5.7 B. Pasternak, *Doctor Zhivago*, 1958, Collins; 6.3(a) Florence Farmborough, *Nurse at the Russian Front: A Diary 1914–18*, Constable Publishers, 1974; 6.3(b) J. Sadoul, *Notes sur la révolution bolchévique*, Libraire François Maspero, Paris, 1971; 6.8(b), 6.8(c) V. Serge, *Year One of the Russian Revolution*, translated by Peter Sedgwick, Allen Lane, The Penguin Press, 1972, translation copyright © Peter Sedgwick, 1972; 6.11 M. Leibman, *Leninism under Lenin*, Merlin Press Ltd, 1975; 6.12 R. Munting, *The Economic Development of the USSR*, Croom Helm, 1982; 7.1 C. E. Bechhofer, *Through Starving Russia*, Methuen & Co., 1921.

Illustration   Photos on p.28, 1.1 from M. Lyons, *Russia in Original Photographs 1860–1920*, 1977; 2.2 Hoover Institution Library; 7.2 The Hulton Picture Company; 7.7(a) Novosti Press Agency.

Every effort has been made to reach copyright holders; the publishers would be pleased to hear from anyone whose rights they have unwittingly infringed.

Cover illustration   *Lenin Proclaiming Soviet Power at the Second Congress of Soviets*, a painting after the event by Vladimir Serov. (David King Collection).

Map   5.4(b) by Jeff Edwards.

Contents

Introduction

Preface

The purpose of this book is to provide students with an introduction to the main historical problems posed by the Russian Revolution. The questions are intended to introduce students to the main events and to lead them to a closer examination of the sources. Those who are more committed to study will ultimately formulate their own questions about the issues raised.

Selections of documents are necessarily edited history but I have tried to give as much context as possible to my selection. The cuts I have made have been usually to avoid repetitious argument. The main victim here has been Lenin, since his style was to try to meet opposing arguments in advance. This led him over the same ground two or three times. I have taken the liberty of sparing the modern-day reader this. All of which highlights the problems of relying on someone else's selection. One must start somewhere, however, and perhaps it would be as well, in this of all subjects, to remind the reader of Karl Marx's favourite motto, 'De omnibus dubitandum' (one should doubt everything)![1]

Key events

The February Revolution, 1917

On International Women's Day, 8 March 1917,[2] the Government of Tsar Nicholas II introduced a new round of bread and flour rationing in the capital, Petrograd (formerly St Petersburg). For the thousands of women, housewives and factory workers, it was the final blow. They ignored the pleas of union leaders to remain calm. The banners carried on that day included more than demands for bread, but also an end to the war and the overthrow of the autocracy. There were no casualties and the day seemed to end peacefully. However, the following day saw a mass strike involving half the factories in Petrograd. The demands for the overthrow of the Tsar now outstripped those for bread. It was on the third day, 10 March, that the police began firing on the striking workers.

By 12 March many of the conscript troops of the Petrograd garrison began to listen to the pleas of the demonstrators. Some remained hesitant, others moved over to join the crowds and fire on the police. The Volhynian Regiment (among others) killed their commander and went over to the workers. A bread riot had become a revolution.

On 12 March, Russia acquired not one, but two, new governments. The Petrograd *Soviet* of Workers Deputies, which had briefly existed during the 1905 Revolution, was revived [1.13]. On the same day, and in the same building, the Tauride Palace, the *Duma* ignored the Tsar's call to disperse, and hesitatingly formed 'a Provisional Committee' [1.10]. This later became known as the Provisional Government. It was the politicians from this group who requested the Tsar's abdication on 15 March. This he did once it was clear that he no longer could enjoy the trust of his army generals. The February Revolution was over. It was regarded as relatively bloodless since only 1,315 people were wounded or killed.

Dual power: the Provisional Government and the Petrograd Soviet

The period between March and November has often been referred to as one of 'dual power'. This is because the Provisional Government, made up of landlords, industrialists and middle-class professionals ('the *bourgeoisie*' in Marxist terms), was nominally regarded as the Government. However, it had not been elected and had no programme. It had hastily summoned itself into being when the Tsar's position appeared hopeless.

The Petrograd Soviet had a greater claim to legitimacy. First formed in November 1905, it had been crushed by the Tsar's troops, and its leaders, including the young Trotsky, had been exiled to Siberia. It had arisen out of the strike committees in each factory in Petrograd, who had sent delegates to the Soviet. It was, of course, only intended for the working class in Petrograd. However, the Soviet movement quickly expanded to include the various garrisons in Petrograd, taking the title 'The Petrograd Soviet of Soldiers and Workers'. Soviets sprang up in other Russian towns too, and even in some country areas amongst the peasantry.

Whilst the Provisional Government nominally governed, it found that in practice it could do nothing without the approval of the Soviet. A clear example of this was over the question of the continuation of the war. The first document issued by the Petrograd Soviet, its 'Order No. 1' [1.14], urged soldiers to obey the Provisional Government 'with the exception of those instances in which they contradict the orders and decrees of the Soviet of Workers' and Soldiers' Deputies'. Further clashes occurred over war aims. Whilst the Soviets stood for ending the war as quickly as possible 'without annexations', the Provisional Government's Foreign Minister, Paul Milyukov, wanted to keep Russia in the war and to continue the fight for the Tsar's war aims [2.4–2.7]. This unleashed a storm of protest and Milyukov resigned in May, under popular pressure led by the Petrograd Soviet.

In fact the members of the Provisional Government were in a difficult, if not impossible, position. The war was deeply unpopular, yet even those who did not share Milyukov's annexationist policy felt duty bound to the *Entente*, whose democratic system they hoped to emulate. Furthermore, the leaders of the Provisional Government had shared the general demand for a Constituent Assembly, but they soon realised that if elections were held, the *Socialist Revolutionaries (SRs)* would win the support of the peasant masses, whilst the gains made by the *Bolsheviks* in the City Duma elections in June showed who the workers in the cities would vote for. Elections were therefore constantly postponed. As the Provisional Government claimed that areas of policy like the redistribution of the land should 'wait for the Constituent Assembly', paralysis was complete.

The Return of Lenin

The Provisional Government was clearly in disarray in the summer of 1917, yet the Soviet was scarcely able to offer any alternative leadership. The Soviet was dominated by the SRs and the *Mensheviks*, both of whom thought that the revolution in Russia should be a bourgeois one. They believed that the role of the Soviet was therefore merely to protect the bourgeois revolution and to look after the interests of the workers and peasants, in the way that a trade union would.

The Bolsheviks in Petrograd, led by Stalin and Kamenev, were, at first, equally confused. They agreed that the Provisional Government should be given support. All this changed with the return of Lenin from his Swiss exile in April 1917 [3.1].

Despite the ecstatic welcome which greeted him, Lenin was impatient with the members of his own Bolshevik Party. He was appalled by their support for the Mensheviks in the Soviet, and the patriotic editorials of Kamenev, which he had read in the Bolshevik Party newspaper, *Pravda* ('Truth'). He brought with him on his 'sealed train' an entirely new view of the future of the Russian Revolution. This view was based on his experience during the First World War.

Lenin and the April Theses

At the beginning of the First World War, Lenin had been deeply shocked by the failure of the *Social Democratic Party* in Germany to oppose the Kaiser's war plans. He even thought that the article in the German socialist paper, *Vorwärts* ('Forwards'), which told of the Social Democrats' vote in favour of the war budget, must be a forgery! This betrayal of internationalist socialist principles proved to Lenin that a new era had dawned in the history of the international working class. In Russia both

Bolsheviks and Mensheviks opposed the war effort and Lenin made the struggle against the war his main activity. For him, the war showed that capitalism was in acute crisis.

In his most famous work *Imperialism: the Highest Stage of Capitalism*, written in 1916, Lenin explained to the workers of Europe that the First World War was an 'imperialist war'. It had been started by the capitalist governments in order to gain new territories which they could exploit as sources of raw materials and as markets. He argued that capitalism had now entered its final stage of decay as a social system – the age of imperialism.

Lenin now concluded that any socialist revolution, wherever it started, would have to be international. It would have to spread to other countries if it was to succeed. This was why he was able to argue in his *Letters from Afar* and the 'April Theses' [3.2] that the task of the Bolshevik Party was not to allow the Provisional Government to run the country: it must win over the majority in the Soviets and govern for the working class. He further advocated the immediate redistribution of land to the peasants and the signing of an immediate peace treaty with Germany. First Lenin had to win over the leading members of his own Party to these ideas. After a series of acrimonious discussions [3.3] he emerged victorious by the beginning of May. He thus gave the Bolsheviks a programme which, summarised in the slogans 'All Power to the Soviets' and 'Bread, Peace and Land', was closest to the deepest desires of the workers and soldiers who were most politically active in 1917.

As a consequence, Bolshevik support in all urban centres increased dramatically as 1917 progressed. In the massive June demonstrations, called by the leaders of the Petrograd Soviet to outmanoeuvre the Bolsheviks, it was the banners carrying Bolshevik slogans which dominated the march.

The July Days, 1917

However, the Bolsheviks were not as radical as some sections of the working class. This was particularly the case in Kronstadt, the huge naval base just ouside Petrograd, where the Soviet was not dominated by any single group. Here the sailors organised their own armed demonstration which carried the Bolshevik's own slogans 'All Power to the Soviets' and 'Down with the Ten Capitalist Ministers'. When the soldiers and sailors brought their demonstration to the centre of Petrograd, the Bolsheviks were placed in a dilemma. They could not condemn it nor could they give it full support [2.12(a)]. They attempted to turn it into a peaceful procession but when shots were fired at the demonstrators, chaos ensued.

The Provisional Government, with the help of the Menshevik and SR majority in the Petrograd Soviet, soon brought in reinforcements and crushed the demonstration. These disorders became known as 'The July Days'. Though the Bolsheviks helped negotiate the disarming and arrest of the sailors, and the abandonment of strategic seizures such as the Peter and Paul Fortress, they were soon blamed for the bloodshed [2.12(b)]. Prime Minister G. Lvov was replaced by Kerensky, a right-wing SR with links to the Soviet [1.10]. Bolshevik newspapers were now closed, warrants were put out for the arrest of the Bolshevik leadership and whilst Lenin and Stalin fled, Kamenev and Trotsky (who chose this moment to join the Bolsheviks) were imprisoned. At the same time the Government tried to discredit the Bolsheviks by claiming that Lenin was a 'German spy'. For a brief period Bolshevik support wavered but there were few resignations from the Party. For Lenin the whole episode demonstrated another step forward in the struggle between the classes in Russia in 1917. He remained in hiding, later moving to Finland, and did not re-emerge until the October Revolution itself. For Kerensky and the members of the Provisional Government it brought relief from the threat from 'the Left'. It also consolidated the Mensheviks and SRs around the Government, as several of their leaders entered the Cabinet. However, the next threat was to come from 'the Right'.

The Kornilov Affair

Despite the failure of the June offensive at the front, despite the entry of Mensheviks into the Government, the Kerensky cabinet remained wedded to the idea of continuing the war. General Kornilov was now appointed Commander in Chief, and the death penalty was restored at the front line. Kerensky supported Kornilov's efforts to restore discipline in the army and tried to demonstrate the new political unity of the country by holding the Moscow State Conference.

Unfortunately for Kerensky, the Conference demonstrated the exact opposite. The Bolsheviks not only boycotted the proceedings but also managed to organise a general strike in the city. The Mensheviks and even the SRs attacked the attempts to restore discipline in the army but had no alternative policy themselves.

As for the Right, they now hailed Kornilov as their hero and openly talked of a military takeover. This was also increasingly attractive to Milyukov and his supporters in the *Kadet* Party. Although still in the Provisional Government, Kadet influence was waning, and so for them dictatorship was becoming preferable to democracy. In such an atmosphere it was not suprising that the Moscow State Conference did no more than give Kerensky another platform for his emotional, patriotic speech-making. It solved nothing.

The actual origins of the 'Kornilovschina', the Kornilov Affair, are confusing. Kornilov always maintained that Kerensky lied about his orders [2.13]. Kornilov claimed that he had been told to bring troops up to Petrograd to continue the policy of restoring order. Kerensky denied ever having allowed this and there is little doubt that in the final analysis Kornilov revolted against his political master. When Kerensky ordered him to halt, Kornilov continued with his preparations to move on Petrograd.

Whatever the debate on the origins of the crisis, there has been little question about who the beneficiaries were. The Bolshevik Party had to be brought back in from the political cold to resist Kornilov since only the Bolsheviks had the confidence of the working class [2.14]. Lenin was not slow to recognise the opportunity for political advance which the Kornilov Revolt presented [3.4]. Although still in a minority in the Soviets, the Bolsheviks took the lead in organising the struggle against Kornilov. They organised a Red Guard amongst the workers, set up a Military Revolutionary Committee (originally dominated by SRs and Mensheviks), secured the release of the Bolsheviks imprisoned in July, and organised the propaganda and fraternisation with Kornilov's troops. This led to the disruption of the railway network and the desertion of most of Kornilov's troops. Kornilov was arrested and the Bolsheviks' support increased even more dramatically. Kornilov's failure only under-lined the increasing isolation and confusion of the Kerensky Government.

The October Revolution, 1917

For Lenin, the Kornilov Affair demonstrated that the Provisional Government was now finished and that the Bolsheviks should themselves begin to organise an insurrection. In August and September more evidence came in to support his view in the shape of elections to the Soviets. In the Petrograd Soviet the Bolsheviks, headed by Trotsky, were able to take over the Executive Committee. However, Lenin's call for insurrection was not answered by other Bolshevik leaders. Throughout the autumn of 1917 Lenin directed a stream of letters to the Bolshevik Central Committee pleading, arguing and cajoling them to prepare for insurrection [3.5]. Even Lenin's threat to resign from the Central Committee seems to have failed to move the other Bolshevik leaders. When they finally did agree, on 23 October, to make the seizure of power 'the order of the day', two of Lenin's oldest comrades, Zinoviev and Kamenev printed their opposition to Lenin in Gorky's newspaper, *Novaya Zhizn* ('New Life') [3.6].

It is an indication of the complacency and weakness of the Kerensky Government that it was not able to resist these well-publicised plans for insurrection. When Kerensky finally did act on 6 November it was to send troops to close off the bridges which led from the Bolshevik stronghold in the factory district of Vyborg to the city centre. However Kerensky's troops were prevented from doing this by troops loyal to the Bolsheviks. The Bolsheviks, led by Trotsky, now began their insurrection. All the main public utilities including the telegraph office and Government buildings were occupied with hardly a shot fired [3.7]. Kerensky fled and tried to rally some Cossack detachments. When they were repulsed, and deserted him, at Gatchina, near Petrograd, he fled into exile.

The Bolshevik Government

The Bolsheviks had come to power promising 'Peace, Bread and Land' and 'All Power to the Soviets'. On peace and land Lenin wasted no time drafting decrees on both in the first two days of the new regime [6.1]. Bread was however a more intractable problem since that was not a matter to be settled by decree [6.3(a) and (b)].

No one had a clear idea as to what 'All Power to the Soviets' meant or how it would operate. Lenin's own views had changed in the course of the previous twelve years and were to change again during the first eight months of Bolshevik rule [4.2 and 4.4]. Allied to this problem were the questions of the Constituent Assembly and the relationship of the Bolsheviks to the other parties which called themselves socialist to some degree [3.9]. On all these issues the Bolsheviks were divided, so their policies were often the product of fudged compromises. One tendency which is clear, however, is that before the signing of the Treaty of Brest-Litovsk in March 1918, the Bolsheviks passed through what is often described as their 'utopian phase'. At this point optimism was at its height and Lenin expressed himself time and again on the capacity of the ordinary masses to administer the new social order. This was given practical force in the Decree on workers' control of the factories. Political prisoners were released if they promised not to attack the Soviet power [4.8a], and the Bolsheviks entered into a coalition with the largest peasant party, the 'Left SRs'.

Parliament or Soviet?

Since the days of Alexander II the opposition to the Tsar was united by the call for a representative assembly. In the 1905 Revolution, Nicholas II had only managed to regain control of the country by offering a parliament or Duma. This was immediately negated by the promulgation of the Fundamental Law of 1906 which maintained that the Tsar remained an autocrat; in other words, the Duma would have no real power. In the first two Dumas the Kadets and after them the Social Democrats tried to contest the Tsar's power and as a result the Dumas were dismissed.

In 1917, the February Revolution was hailed by all opposition parties as the beginning of the long awaited 'democratic revolution'. However, the various Provisional Governments continuously delayed holding a Constituent Assembly until the war was over. Milyukov, the Kadet leader, realised that an election for such an assembly would have given a majority to the socialist parties (as eventually happened) and thus was in favour of delay until the war was over. This meant that the Provisional Government ruled with a rather dubious legitimacy, especially when faced with the Petrograd Soviet which could claim to be a popularly elected body.

But if the democrats were slow to bring democracy, the attitude of the Bolsheviks was equally ambiguous. Once the April Theses became the basis of Bolshevik thinking, the slogan 'All Power to the Soviets' should have rendered calls for a Constituent Assembly redundant. However this was not the case. Bolshevik demands throughout 1917 continuously called for both, and the Bolsheviks went ahead with the elections for the Constituent Assembly, held on 13 November. However, these elections were based on arrangements made under the Provisional Government and came too early for the Bolshevik policies on peace and land to affect the result. Predictably the Bolsheviks swept the urban working class, but the Right SRs, with the peasant vote, held the majority [4.5]. The Constituent Assembly met on 18 January 1918. It refused to support Soviet power or the Bolshevik Government. After a mammoth sitting it was dispersed by troops loyal to the Bolsheviks and Left SRs, and delegates were locked out from subsequent sessions [4.6 and 4.7]. Though the Right SRs tried to organise demonstrations in support of the Assembly, these had little backing and were easily dispersed.

Terror and revolution

If the Constituent Assembly's dissolution was relatively simple, the Bolsheviks were soon faced with new threats. After the Bolsheviks had signed the Treaty of Brest-Litovsk in March 1918, the Left SRs attempted to disrupt the treaty by murdering the German ambassador, Count Mirbach. At the same time they launched an insurrection in Moscow. The Left SR members of the *Cheka* who carried out the assassination of Mirbach were later shot and the incident marked the end of the Left SR's tentative support for the Bolsheviks in the Soviets. Now they, like the Right SRs, undertook a campaign of terrorism which mirrored that of their *Populist* predecessors in the time of the Tsars. Leading Bolsheviks like the popular orator, Volodarsky, had already been murdered by the SRs, and an important member of the Bolshevik party, Uritsky, was killed in August. Lenin and Bukharin both survived attempts on their lives. The attack on Lenin undoubtedly hastened the collapse of his health in 1922.

These assassinations opened up a new phase exemplified by the 'Red Terror'. Hitherto much of the violence against Bolshevik enemies had been either spontaneous, or it had been more rhetoric than action. For example, the Kadets had been banned and their leaders accused of treason but their paper continued to appear throughout the summer of 1918. But after September 1918 there was a massive crackdown in which an untold number of opponents of the Bolsheviks were shot. According to *Izvestia* ('News', the paper of the Petrograd Soviet) the total number executed in Petrograd during the terror was eight hundred.[3] Most of the victims seem to have been selected for their former role under the Tsar or their membership of the possessing classes.

Towards the other socialist parties the suppression of freedom seems to have had many ups and downs [4.11(b)]. This was probably because the Mensheviks and SRs both had splits and fluctuating policies towards the Bolshevik Government. The Mensheviks announced in October 1918 that they accepted the October revolution, but demanded an end to the revolutionary tribunals and the terror [4.9]. Lenin, at this point, asked no more of the Mensheviks than 'neutrality and good neighbour relations'. Both Mensheviks and SRs were welcomed back into the Soviets so long as they gave no support to the armies ranged against Soviet Russia. Once again the SRs split into separate groups, some pledged to armed struggle against the Bolsheviks.

Both parties, Menshevik and SR, continued to have a political life in 'Red Russia' right until December 1920, when they attended (but without voting rights) the 8th All-Russian Congress of the Soviets. The Kronstadt Revolt of March 1921 (not to be confused with the Kronstadt demonstration of 1917, see page 7) was not only to kill off all legal opposition outside the Bolshevik Party but also made it difficult for opposition to flourish as it had done traditionally within the Party itself.

Brest-Litovsk

The Bolshevik view of the development of the revolution was intimately connected to the war and the future international workers' revolution which Lenin believed would issue from it. The war had caused the revolutionary crisis of 1917 in Russia and no government which continued the war could exist for long. Hence the Decree on Peace was issued on the first day of Soviet power in November 1917 [5.1] and by December an armistice had been signed with the Germans. Lenin was for signing the quickest possible peace at any price since Russia had no army in the real sense and the Germans had already established themselves in the Baltic provinces within a short distance of Petrograd.

However, as on economic and political issues, the Bolsheviks were divided. This was all too clearly emphasised in December 1917 when

Joffe brought back the first peace offer from Brest-Litovsk (the Polish town where the German Eastern Command had its headquarters). Russia was to agree to the independence of former Russian territory in Poland, Lithuania, Courland, and parts of Estonia and Latvia. Whilst Lenin was quite sanguine about these demands of the 'German imperialists' [5.2(a)], the Left Communists, led by Bukharin, the leader of the Moscow Bolsheviks, demanded that the war should continue in order to assist the German workers and thus promote international revolution. When Lenin asked them with what forces they proposed to continue the fight, Bukharin advocated moving the seat of government beyond the Urals and carrying out a guerrilla campaign in the territories occupied by the German army [5.2(b)]. But as Lenin pointed out, this would mean that the Bolsheviks would also be abandoning their own bases amongst the working classes of Petrograd and Moscow.

Trotsky, as Commissar for Foreign Affairs, had already revolutionised diplomacy by publishing the secret treaties which the Tsar had signed with Britain and France. He not only sent a Note to the Entente governments of Britain and France, as well as the USA, pleading with them to join the peace negotiations at Brest (something they had already refused to do) but had also tried less orthodox channels by negotiating with the unofficial representatives of Britain and France for possible military aid. Whilst these representatives all advocated assistance to the Bolsheviks, they were ignored by their own governments. Indeed plans to send aid to the *Whites* had already been made.

Trotsky decided to conduct the negotiations himself. He dragged out the negotiations until 10 February, when, to the utter astonishment of the Central Powers, he left Brest-Litovsk offering neither war nor peace. The Bolshevik delegation returned to Petrograd where they were greeted as heroes. However, the hope that Trotsky held, that a further German advance would lead to revolution in Germany, was soon shattered [5.3]. The Germans advanced over 150 miles in less than a week and were soon threatening Petrograd. On 24 February, despite hostile opposition on all sides, the Central Committee of the Bolshevik Party voted by 7 to 4 (with 4 abstentions, including Trotsky's) to accept the new, even more draconian, peace terms. The Treaty of Brest-Litovsk was duly signed on 3 March 1918 [5.4].

Now the Soviet Republic abandoned all claim to the bulk of the Ukraine, as well as all of Poland and the Baltic states. The Bolsheviks signed away 55 million people (26% of the population), 75% of the railway network, 26% of the iron and steel production and most of the best land that had formerly belonged to the Russian Empire. Lenin's own attitude was that the world revolution would arrive soon to sweep the provisions of all treaties aside. Until then 'I don't mean to read it and I don't mean to fulfil it except in so far as I am forced'.[4]

From Imperialist War to Civil War

Lenin's slogan in 1915 had been 'Turn the imperialist war into a civil war'. The Russian working class had done just this but, although Brest-Litovsk brought peace with Germany, it did not end the imperialist war. The previous allies of Tsarist Russia (the 'Entente Powers', Britain and France) aided by the United States, Japan, and the newly independent states of Poland, Finland, Estonia, Latvia and Lithuania, all declared war on Bolshevik Russia. They not only gave active assistance to the Whites, the various armies led by ex-Tsarist officers like Admiral Kolchak, Generals Yudenich, Denikin and Wrangel, but they also took over parts of Russia. The Japanese established themselves in Vladivostok, the British and Americans in Archangel and Murmansk, and the French in the Crimea. The aim of this intervention was ostensibly to bring about a government which would re-open the war with Germany. However this rationale was less convincing after November 1918 when the armistice brought the First World War to an end. Allied intervention continued for another two years and was a major contributor to the continuation of the civil war until December, 1920.

In fact this intervention nearly swung the military balance against the Bolsheviks. In October 1919, Yudenich almost took Petrograd, and the Bolshevik leadership seriously discussed the possibility of returning to an underground struggle. However, with the relief of Petrograd [5.10(b)] the tide turned and the Whites were on the retreat. Indeed, when Pilsudski, the Polish leader, with the encouragement of the Entente, launched an attack on the Ukraine in 1920, the Red Army not only repelled it but actually advanced to the gates of Warsaw.

At this point Lenin had hoped the Polish workers would rise up and join their Russian comrades to bring the working class revolution closer to Germany. Trotsky had argued against the advance into Poland since he believed it would only lead the Polish workers to identify with Pilsudski. He was proved to be correct and the Red Army was driven back. The subsequent Treaty of Riga was very favourable to Poland. Henceforth the Bolsheviks looked only to the Communist International, which had been founded in January 1919, to spread world revolution by political rather than military means.

From War Communism to New Economic Policy

The Bolsheviks had arrived at power in a predominantly peasant country with an economy ruined to the point of exhaustion by 4 years of war. To deal with this the Bolsheviks only had Lenin's few remarks in the 'April Theses' [3.2] as a programme for dealing with the economy. Lenin had announced that the aim was to proceed with the building of a 'socialist order' (a workers' controlled state inside Russia). He had also envisaged that the international revolution would, within a matter of months rather than years, ensure the victory of the *proletarian* revolution in Russia.

However, the Bolsheviks soon found that they could not simply administer a capitalist economy whilst awaiting the world revolution. To begin with, factory owners and bank workers actively tried to sabotage the economy and refused to co-operate with the Bolsheviks [6.7]. Furthermore, the working classes themselves did not wait for the Bolsheviks, but began demanding the appropriation of their own factories [6.8].

The greatest danger that faced the Bolsheviks was the starvation of the population which was already severe at the beginning of 1918 [6.3]. The Bolsheviks blamed this on hoarding of grain by rich peasants and speculators. Requisitioning squads from the towns were set up to unearth this supposed surplus. These gradually drew the Bolsheviks into a civil war with the peasants in the countryside which was to last as long as the struggle against the Whites. It was only abandoned in March 1921 [6.4–6.6]. This policy never solved the food crisis and indeed worsened it [7.1 and 7.2]. As a result many workers who were not already fighting in the Red Army abandoned the cities in search of food [6.10 and 6.11]. Increasingly it was the Bolshevik Party that had to take on the role which had originally been ascribed to the working class as a whole, the 'dictatorship of the proletariat'. (In *Marxist* theory, all states are dictatorships, since all are instruments used by one class to suppress another. Thus Parliament is the expression of the dictatorship of the bourgeoisie, and the Soviets were seen by Lenin as the dictatorship of the proletariat.) In the period of the civil war, state direction began to replace local workers' initiatives, and nationalisation was now seen as the same thing as 'socialism'. With the economy in ruins by 1921, however, it was clear that what Lenin now called 'war communism' would have to be abandoned [6.12 and 7.3].

The Kronstadt Revolt, 1921

Lenin had already planned a new economic policy which he described as 'a retreat to state capitalism', to be announced at the Tenth Party Congress, when the Kronstadt Revolt broke out. Hitherto the most militant and loyal supporters of the workers' revolution, the soldiers and sailors of Kronstadt, now called for fresh elections to the Soviets, legalisation of all socialist parties and the reintroduction of the free market (which Lenin had already decided to do) [7.5]. The Bolsheviks believed that the Whites were behind the revolt and refused to negotiate seriously [7.8]. They were particularly worried that, when the ice around the island where the naval base was located melted, this would allow Allied ships to enter the mouth of the River Neva, threatening Petrograd. Not without a great deal of difficulty, they managed to organise assaults on Kronstadt and, at the second attempt, they managed to storm it [7.6 and 7.7]. This was in March 1921. For many historians this represents another convenient dividing line in the history of the Russian Revolution. Not only was it the month of the Kronstadt Revolt, but at the Tenth Party Congress the Russian Communist Party adopted what was later known as the *New Economic Policy* (NEP) which involved de-nationalisation of smaller factories and the re-establishment of the free market, particularly in agricultural produce [7.4]. It led to a slow revival of the economy over the next few years, and was to be the economic policy of the Russian state until Stalin's collectivisation drive and the Five Year Plans, which began in 1928.

Equally significantly, March 1921 saw the failure of the German communists to seize power in the 'March Action'. Although there was to be a further attempt by the communists to seize power in Germany in November 1923, this was in fact the last independent action of the German communists. Like the defeat of the Red Army before Warsaw in 1920, it was a nail in the coffin of the international revolution which the Bolsheviks had counted on to be able to build socialism. The question now was how could the Soviet Union exist in a hostile capitalist world. This question was still unanswered at the time of the death of Lenin. The Third (Communist) International now began to adopt policies which were the very opposite of those the Bolsheviks had espoused to win power in Russia.

In January 1922 Lenin suffered his first stroke and his contribution until his death in January 1924 was only sporadic. His later writings are dotted with references to the growth of bureaucracy and his final so-called Testament called for the removal of Stalin from his post as General Secretary of the Party [7.12]. The latter was only saved by the intervention of Zinoviev who was later to be shot by Stalin after the show trials of the 1930s. Lenin himself, despite his own wishes, had his body embalmed and placed on public view in a tomb in Red Square, Moscow. It was the beginning of 'the cult of personality' which Kruschev denounced in his speech to the 20th Party Congress in 1956. It was certainly a long way from the ideals for which Lenin, the Bolsheviks and the Russian working class had fought in 1917.

The historical issues

The causes and nature of the Russian Revolution

Was revolution inevitable in Russia in 1917? Historians are naturally reluctant to say that anything was inevitable, but in retrospect it is possible to argue that Tsarist Russia had by 1917 arrived at an impasse. The war which had in 1914 brought a wave of patriotic support for the Tsar had long since ceased to be other than a source of misery for the soldiers and the increasingly hungry populace. As in the war against Japan in 1904–5, Russia was inadequately prepared in 1914 and had, by the end of August, suffered a series of heavy defeats from which the army never recovered. Despite superior manpower resources, despite success against the Austro-Hungarian armies, including the initially successful Brusilov Offensive of May–June 1916, it was all the Russian Army could do to hold the Eastern Front against the German Empire until 1917. Two and a half million Russian soldiers died in holding the line from Riga to Rumania for almost two and a half years.

In 1915 the Tsar had himself taken over the command of the Army at the Front. This did not help the war effort and left the Government in Petrograd largely in the hands of his wife, Tsarina Alexandra, a religious hysteric who fervently believed in both autocratic rule and the advice of the 'holy man' Gregory Rasputin. Rasputin's pernicious advice brought 22 changes of minister in about as many months. Many of his choices, if not actually pro-German, certainly hoped for a peace. His assassination in December 1916 by monarchists and members of the Royal family did not end talk of a palace revolution to replace Nicholas. In the event the series of political strikes which had been building up since 1915 exploded into the food riots and strike wave of February, 1917. Tsarism, having promised reforms in 1905 to get out of a similar situation, had nothing to offer this time. The Parliament or Duma which had been created in 1905 as an experiment in constitutional monarchy had been reduced to a rubber stamp by 1907. Even so the Tsar's first act in the face of the February crisis of 1917 was to attempt to dissolve it.

How far was the war responsible for the fall of Tsarism? As Geoffrey Hosking wrote in his recent study *A History of the Soviet Union* (1985) this is an 'open question'. Certainly the Tsar seems to have learned few lessons from the near-disaster of 1904–5. He consistently fired or distrusted able ministers like Witte and Stolypin, replacing them with self-confessed incompetents like Goremykin; he refused to recognise the Duma as a future partner in government and changed the electoral laws to give a massive over-representation to the nobility. All this at a time when Russia was experiencing an industrial revolution every bit as dramatic as that in early nineteenth century Britain. But Russia had survived twelve years of these problems before the privations of two years of war brought about a spontaneous explosion of a starving and war weary people. It cannot be said that the war reduced Nicholas II's room for manoeuvre since he did not recognise that his regime was in danger until the final blow came. It did however reduce the possibilities open to those politicians, like Milyukov, who wished to preserve the monarchy in some form. The continuation of the crisis of government after the fall of the Tsar was precisely because no government before the Bolsheviks felt able to abandon the aims for which Russia had entered the war.

Marxism and the Russian Revolution

The majority of the revolutionary parties opposing Tsarism were influenced to some degree or other by the theories of the German thinker, Karl Marx (1818–83). Marx was not the originator of communist or socialist ideas (he used the words interchangeably). Ideas about a co-operative society which was run for the benefit of those who produced its wealth had appeared in the later Middle Ages.[5] The original contribution of Marx was to explain the struggle for communism as part of an inevitable historical process which would one day see the industrial working class (or proletariat) defeat the capitalist class (or bourgeoisie) who owned for themselves the means of production such as factories and estates. Once victorious, the proletariat would go on to establish communism, a society of 'freely-associated producers', without a state, police, money, national frontiers or the exploitation of one human being by another. For Marx communism was the final stage of history which could only be reached after society had passed through ancient slave society, medieval feudalism and modern industrial capitalism. Marx had written these ideas with Friedrich Engels, in *The Communist Manifesto* in 1848. After this he spent twenty years analysing the workings of the capitalist economy which led to the production of his great work *Capital* (1867). He left no blueprint of communist society since he regarded such schemes as historically worthless. Instead he left a series of scattered comments which his followers could interpret in different ways. This was to prove particularly significant for the Russian socialist movement.

Socialist Opposition in Tsarist Russia

Russian socialism had developed in two broad movements from the 1880s onwards, and by the beginning of the twentieth century these movements had taken on clear forms as the Socialist Revolutionary Party and the Russian Social Democratic Labour Party, a Marxist party. The Socialist Revolutionaries, or SRs, were a loose confederation who saw the ancient peasant commune or *mir* as the basis of a specific Russian kind of socialism. They thus argued that Russia could proceed to socialism without having to experience the horrors of industrialisation. Marxism was introduced by Russian intellectuals like George Plekhanov. In 1883 he founded the group 'The Liberation of Labour' which waged a literary war against the forerunners of the SRs, the narodniks (or Populists). It attracted a number of young intellectuals to Marxism including Vladimir Ulyanov or Lenin. Lenin distinguished himself in 1899 by publishing

The Development of Capitalism in Russia which statistically demonstrated that Russia was developing capitalism anyway and that therefore the proletariat, and not the peasantry would be the agent of revolutionary change. Lenin was able to develop this theory in the leisure of Siberian exile (1895–1900) and, whilst he was there, an embryonic Russian Social Democratic Labour Party had come into existence in 1898. However, Russia's economic and political backwardness did pose problems for Russian marxists and this led to a split in the Social Democratic Labour Party in 1903. Lenin's opponents took the name Mensheviks (the Minority) whilst his own followers became known as the Bolsheviks (the Majority). There were a number of differences between them. The Mensheviks wished to have a large political party of workers, imitating the large German Social Democratic Party with its millions of members and its own trades union organisations. Lenin opposed this: he pointed out that Germany was very different because a mass party could exist legally there, whereas in Russia the Social Democratic Party was illegal. He and the Bolsheviks wanted a party of committed and professional revolutionaries who would be tightly-knit and disciplined to resist the *Okhrana*, the Tsar's secret police.

But the two groups were also split on the future course of Russia's development. They agreed on the need for a revolution to overthrow the Tsar and, until the First World War, they even agreed that the revolution would be 'bourgeois democratic' in character. In other words, that the overthrow of the Tsar would lead to a parliamentary democracy which would oversee the further development of Russian capitalism. They did not agree on how long this parliamentary democracy would have to last. Whilst the Mensheviks talked in terms of decades, Lenin wrote of an 'uninterrupted revolution' which would very quickly lead to a workers' socialist state.

During the First World War Lenin published *Imperialism – the Highest Stage of Capitalism*, in which he drew the conclusion that capitalism everywhere had had its day. This was even true for economically backward Russia which was still in the early stages of industrialisation. Even so, Russia was now, in 1914, the world's sixth industrial power with a working class the size of Great Britain's. Despite the danger of isolation amongst a predominantly peasant economy, this working class would be able to take power, and hold it, as part of an international workers' revolution. This view was not only to have consequences for the decisive actions of the Bolsheviks in 1917 but also has helped to fuel the debate about the reasons for the emergence of the Stalinist regime after the Revolution.

Menshevik historians, like R. R. Abramovitch, argue that, by trying to establish socialism before Russia was a fully developed capitalist state,

Lenin broke with the Marxist conception of history which saw every society passing through feudalism, then capitalism, before socialism could be established. The Russia of 1917, they maintain, was only just passing from a feudal monarchy to a bourgeois republic. Marxists should have supported the Provisional Government since the struggle for democracy had to come before the struggle for socialism. The failure of the Russian Revolution to establish the classless, communist society Marx envisaged, they argue, was simply a result of Lenin's attempt to leap over a whole and inevitable stage of history.

Lenin dismissed these arguments (which were also put forward by leading Bolsheviks like Kamenev) as 'mechanical marxism'. In the age of imperialism the struggle for socialism should not be seen in terms of a single country's struggle, but as a global struggle. It is a debate which even with the benefit of hindsight historians have never been able to resolve.

Kerensky and the July Days

In the non-marxist camp much of the debate has focused on the failure of the Provisional Government to establish itself. This debate centred around the histrionic second Prime Minister of the Provisional Government, Alexander Kerensky. Uniquely placed by virtue of his membership of both the Provisional Government and the Petrograd Soviet, Kerensky had become Prime Minister after the July Days. This demonstration has been a source of much controversy. Anti-Bolshevik historians insist that it was a demonstration of the *putschist* tendencies of the Bolsheviks which only failed because they struck too early. However, more recent research by Alexander Rabinowitch[6] shows that the affair was a great embarrassment for the Bolshevik leadership. They found that rank and file Bolsheviks had joined *anarchists* and other groups in an armed demonstration, and despite their attempts to keep the July demonstration peaceful, bloodshed had followed.

Although the July Days made Kerensky Prime Minister, he was to occupy the post for only three months. Whilst his critics have argued that he was personally too weak and too dictatorial to sustain the Government, he has himself, in a series of memoirs, robustly blamed the Soviet Parties (the Mensheviks and SRs), who were too frightened to lose their support amongst the masses by more openly supporting him. He also blamed the supposedly democratic Kadets who rallied to Kornilov in the autumn of 1917. However, it was the issue of the war which really isolated Kerensky from the Soviet parties. His insistence on fighting to victory meant that he had to turn to the army. When the latter showed a preference for Kornilov, Kerensky had no real support left.

The October Revolution

Was this a popular rising, or a putsch by a small body of determined politicians? The answer to this question usually depends on the political standpoint of the observer. Historians on the Left, like Marcel Liebman, stress the fact that the Kerensky government could muster no popular, and very little military, support, and that the Bolsheviks had won four-fifths of the votes in the elections to the Second All-Russian Congress of Soviets. This Congress naturally endorsed the overthrow of the Provisional Government. They can also point to the fact that there was little violence in October with few casualties in Petrograd compared with the hundreds that were killed in February.

Historians on the Right, led by Leonard Schapiro, stress the fact that the October Revolution was carried out as a military operation led by Trotsky and that the popular uprising that had characterised the February rising was missing. They also point to the fact that Lenin refused to compromise with the other socialist parties after the overthrow of Kerensky and argue that he was intent on a Bolshevik Party dictatorship from the beginning.

Such diversity only underlines the point that history is not just about digging up 'facts' but is an activity which involves evaluating evidence in order to reach defensible conclusions.

Bolshevik Russia

There are a number of issues about Bolshevik rule which have divided historians. Why, having declared that Soviets would form the basis of the new socialist republic, did the Bolsheviks carry on with the plan to hold elections to the Constituent Assembly only a fortnight after the October Revolution? The elections came too soon to be a judgement on the October Revolution, as can be seen from the fact that the SR manifesto for the Constituent Assembly elections did not even mention it. Furthermore, the October Revolution had split the SRs. Whilst the Right walked out of the Second Congress of Soviets, the Left under Boris Kamkov and Maria Spiridonova had remained and were eventually to enter the Council of People's Commissars. But the holding of the Constituent Assembly elections before this split was formalised meant that the Left SRs were greatly under-represented in the Constituent Assembly. This left the Right SRs with a majority in the Assembly which they would probably not have enjoyed (given that the Left SRs had an overwhelming majority in the elections to the peasant Soviets a few weeks later).

Lenin always maintained that the Bolsheviks did not want to postpone the elections for the Constituent Assembly because this had already been done several times by the Provisional Government and the Bolsheviks had included early elections as one of their slogans. He claimed that he knew that by allowing early elections for the Constituent Assembly the SRs would have a majority by virtue of the peasant vote. However, he argued that this would give the Bolsheviks the chance to show the working class that the SRs were against Soviet rule. This duly happened and the Constituent Assembly was shut down by troops loyal to the Bolsheviks without any significant opposition. However, it was a propaganda gift to the international enemies of the October Revolution who were able to portray Lenin as a dictator to their own working classes.

In the last analysis the only explanation for holding the elections seems to lie in the divisions amongst the Bolshevik leaders themselves. Whilst those on the Left supported Lenin, those on the Right of the Party like Kamenev had hoped to use the Constituent Assembly for some compromise with the other socialist parties. In the event the elections only heightened the fact that Russia was divided into two irreconcilable camps.

These divisions could also be seen over the Treaty of Brest-Litovsk where Bukharin's Left Communist faction argued that it would be a betrayal of the international revolution to make peace with the Kaiser since Germany was ripe for revolution. If the war was prolonged then Germany would join Russia as a workers' state. Some historians today maintain that Bukharin was correct (especially since revolution broke out in Germany in November, 1918, only eight months after Brest-Litovsk). Some also argue that Lenin was signing away his internationalist principles at Brest-Litovsk and that the Treaty represented the end of the 'heroic stage' of the October Revolution. However Lenin always made it clear that he saw the issue as one over which the Bolsheviks had no choice. The Tsar and Kerensky had been toppled because they did not bring peace and it was the promise of peace which had brought the Bolsheviks to power. Even had they refused the German terms they had no army with which to resist.

The Civil War and Allied Intervention

The signing of Brest-Litovsk might have got the Bolsheviks out of the world war but it plunged them into a new war against the 'Whites'. The Bolsheviks had no army and the territory over which their jurisdiction ran was reduced to the central Russian area between Petrograd and Moscow. Their opponents also enjoyed the financial and military support of the Allied Powers, initially intent on keeping Russia in the war, and later in crushing Bolshevism. How were they able to defeat the fourteen armies backed by foreign powers that were at one time ranged against them?

Part of the answer lies in the fact that their enemies were so dispersed and had such divided leadership. There was no co-ordinated strategy between Kolchak in Siberia, Denikin in the Crimea and Yudenich in the Baltic Provinces. And there were examples of clashes between anti-Bolshevik forces. Admiral Kolchak, for example, on capturing the Siberian town of Omsk, executed the SR government he found there, despite the fact that they too were opposed to the Bolsheviks.

At the same time the Bolsheviks enjoyed better communications since most of the Russian railway network was within the territory they held. Trotsky utilised this to the full and soon distinguished himself as an indefatigable and ruthless military organiser. He not only formed a Red Army from virtually nothing but even managed to persuade his suspicious colleagues in the Communist Party that trained leadership could be provided by recruiting into it ex-Tsarist officers. Against objections that these professional soldiers would be politically unreliable he came up with the idea of the commissar, a political watchdog who would accompany each officer. The system was a success and many ex-Tsarist officers, including General Brusilov, increasingly saw the Red Army as the national army against a White army assisted by foreigners.

However the defeat of the Whites did not solve all the problems of the Reds. The Bolsheviks had lost most of the best grain lands of the old Russian Empire at Brest-Litovsk. Grain requisitioning in 'Red' areas was deeply unpopular and led to a civil war within the civil war. However most peasants grew to see the Bolshevik government as less of a threat since the Whites not only requisitioned grain but brought back the former landlords. The latter insisted on the punishment of the peasants so it is not surprising that, despite opposition to grain requisitioning, the peasants largely rallied to the Reds.

The final reason for the ultimate victory of the Bolsheviks was the fact that, by the end of 1920, the Entente powers had withdrawn their support for the Whites.

Nevertheless, the price of victory in the civil war was high. Freedoms had to be abandoned as the Cheka, or secret police, sought out saboteurs; the Soviets met increasingly rarely; elections ceased to be held; and the desperate need to feed the urban population led to the introduction of 'war communism'. 'War communism' was not a systematic plan (the name was only used after it had been abandoned) but consisted of a series of ad hoc measures such as the nationalisation of factories (mainly after their owners had abandoned them) and the requisitioning of grain. The latter had not solved Russia's economic problems and by 1921 famine haunted the Revolution.

Was 'war communism' a success or failure? Some historians would argue that 'war communism' was a success since it enabled the Bolsheviks to hold on until the civil war against the Whites was won. Others regard it as a disaster since Russia's production in virtually every conceivable commodity was more than halved compared with the 1913

figure. However, much of this damage had already been done before
1918, so the statistical argument is hard to maintain.

What 'war communism' failed to do was to keep the working class in
the towns, and this mass exodus to the countryside in search of food had
enormous political consequences for a regime which based itself on the
urban working class. The original revolutionary workers had, by 1921,
either been killed or dispersed fighting in the Red Army, or had returned
to the countryside from the starving towns. The result was to change the
relationship of the Party with the rest of the working class. From being a
mass workers' party in October 1917, it grew into a huge apparatus
which increasingly supplanted the dying organs of workers' democracy,
the Soviet and factory committees. The supporters of the Bolsheviks
argue that this was the result of the decline of the working class in the
civil war, whilst their opponents argue that it was a result of a deliberate
policy to create a Party dictatorship.

Kronstadt and the Counter-Revolution

The revolt which broke out at Kronstadt in 1921 has been seen by many
(particularly anarchist historians) as a significant turning point in the
revolution. Kronstadt had been the vanguard of the revolution since
early 1917. Sailors from the naval base there had been ready to
implement the Bolshevik programme in July 1917 when the Bolsheviks
themselves had judged it too soon for a second revolution. This only
underlines the point that the Bolsheviks, although supported by the
Kronstadt sailors, never actually controlled them. In March 1921, when
the civil war was over and workers in Petrograd had gone on strike
against economic privation, the Kronstadt sailors became the vanguard
demanding a restoration of Soviet power and new elections to the
Soviets. The Bolsheviks found themselves in the grip of a dilemma. To
have held elections then would have been to bring back the SRs. The SRs
were a peasant party opposed to Soviet power. As the working class were
now largely exhausted and demoralised as a result of the starvation
caused by the civil war, they would have been unable to resist an SR
counter-revolution. The Bolsheviks believed that if they could hold on to
state power, world revolution would come to aid them. So the Bolsheviks
opted for the suppression of the Kronstadt revolt by force and in so doing
broke with their own aim of creating a state run by workers.

At the same time factions like the Workers' Opposition were banned
within the Communist Party. Although in practice factions continued to
exist until the Stalinist era, it was another step on the road to a
totalitarian state dominated by a single party responsible only to one
centre of power. With Stalin established as its General Secretary in 1922

the control of patronage which he wielded enabled him to ensure that his own creatures would be advanced to that centre of decision-making. Such were the roots of dictatorship. There is thus a case for arguing that the Bolsheviks themselves, when faced with international isolation, became the unwilling agents of the very counter-revolution that they had fought against from 1917 to 1921.

The Revolutions of 1917 opened up a new era of hope for a free and socially just society, not just in Russia, but throughout the world. However, by 1928 this vision had all but collapsed under the dictatorship of Stalin. In the 1930s his Show Trials and labour camps and the liquidation of millions of Russians, starting with those who were the most convinced communists, have often been portrayed as the inevitable outcome of the Bolshevik Revolution. This is an ahistorical conclusion since the Russia of the 1920s was still a relatively open society in which the poetry of Mayakovsky, Mandelstam and Blok, the writing of Gorky, the cinema of Eisenstein and the art of Chagall, Malevich and Lisitsky all flourished. It was also a society (at least until 1927) in which debates about the future of Russia were tolerated. Lenin may have left a flawed legacy but Stalinism had roots all of its own in the particular situation of the late 1920s. The question remains, at which point the hopes of the Russian Revolution were shattered. Was it November 1917 when the Bolsheviks came to power, as the Mensheviks would argue? Was it 1918 when the Treaty of Brest-Litovsk was signed? Was it 1921 when the Kronstadt Revolt tried to spark off a 'third revolution' as many anarchists claim, or was it 1924 when Lenin died, as many Trotskyists claim? The turning-point in Red Russia's fortunes cannot be pinned down to a particular event, and the issue of revolution and counter-revolution remains controversial.

The sources and the historiography

The Russian Revolution was arguably the most important event of this century. Its consequences remain with us. This has added an extra dimension of interest to its study. The usual warnings about being aware of the political and social prejudices of historians apply even more strongly when discussing the origins of the system of government of a present-day world power.

However, the 'iron curtain' in academic study of the Russian Revolution did not begin with the Cold War of the 1950s. As A. J. P. Taylor has pointed out, the iron curtain descended in 1918 when the Russian Revolution was attacked by the Allied forces, and it continued in the 1920s with Russia's virtual total isolation from world affairs. During this period little was published in the West except the memoirs of ex-tsarist generals like Denikin (a volume called *The Russian Turmoil* published in

London in 1922) or extremely right-wing histories such as that of Claude Anet *La Révolution russe* (in 3 volumes, Paris 1917–19). The Mensheviks in exile kept up a lively series of publications from their archive in Berlin to add to the generally anti-Bolshevik view.

In Russia, which changed its name from the Russian Socialist Federal Soviet Republics to the Union of Soviet Socialist Republics in 1923, the 1920s represent something of a golden period for historical study before the victory of Stalin suppressed not only much of the history of the Revolution but also, in many cases, the historians. Before then though, Trotsky had written his brilliant and stimulating history of the events up to the Bolshevik takeover[7] and many other participants in the revolution had produced their own reminiscences. The most prominent Bolshevik memoirs produced before 1930 were those of Shlyapnikov, Lenin's widow, Krupskaya, and the brothers Raskolnikov and Ilyin-Zhenevsky.[8] However, the two most valuable eyewitnesses to the events were not members of Lenin's party. The first of these was N. N. Himmer (Sukhanov), a member of the Menshevik Party. His translator, Joel Carmichael, tells us that Sukhanov's memoir 'was required reading in party circles and considered an indispensable source-book for the study of the revolution'. Yet by the end of the 1920s it was no longer referred to, and Sukhanov, who had worked loyally for the Russian state, became one of the first victims of Stalin's purges in 1931. The same fate befell the other great eyewitness account of the Revolution, John Reed's *Ten Days that Shook the World*. On its publication in 1919 Lenin called it 'a truthful and most vivid exposition of the events' which he recommended to the workers of the world. The victory of Stalin in 1928, however, ensured that the book which highlights Trotsky's role and mentions Stalin once, was banned. Today, Reed's book is tolerated in the USSR, but because it highlights Trotsky's significance in the October Revolution, it is not required reading.

The period of Stalinism saw only further suppression of the historical record. Stalin's falsification of the photographic record is notorious (see *The Independent Magazine* 10 December 1988), but he also doctored the written word. The full edition of Lenin's *Collected Works* has to this day not been published in the Soviet Union. Lenin's *Testament* was first published by the American Trotskyist Max Eastman in the 1920s and has never been published in the Soviet Union where its authenticity is still doubted.

The gradual revelation of the truth about Stalin's Soviet Union did little to throw clarity on the history of the Russian Revolution. Now the search was on to prove that the origins of Stalinism lay in the Bolshevik theories of 1917 or in the authoritarian character of Lenin. Symptomatic of the Cold War were the two biographies of Lenin which appeared just after the Second World War by David Shub[9] and Christopher Hill[10]. Both tried to show that Lenin was the direct precursor of Stalin, the former to discredit Lenin, the latter to glorify Stalin. This does not rule them out as sources but they should be handled with care.

A more scrupulous approach was adopted by E. H. Carr in arguably the most important volumes to appear on the Russian Revolution since the Second World War. Carr began life as a diplomat and came late to academic history. His original intention was to write a history of the Soviet Union beginning at the death of Lenin. However he soon found this was inadequate and pushed his researches further back into Russian history. The result was the three-volume work *The Bolshevik Revolution 1917–21*, the first appearing in London in 1956. Carr's work is distinguished by the fact that he made every effort to understand the theoretical and political motivations of the Bolsheviks, particularly Lenin. Carr's work remains the fullest source of information on the Bolshevik Revolution and its causes to date, although its more thematic treatment makes it a difficult work for the uninitiated. For an alternative view, L. Schapiro's *Origin of the Communist Autocracy* is a typical product of the period.

As the Russian revolution approached its first half century, historians seem at last to have considered it worth substantial historical study. A plethora of books on a wide variety of aspects of the Revolution have been published and it is not possible to mention all of them here. The following are noteworthy. There are the two books of Marc Ferro which have both been translated into English[11] dealing with the previously neglected social aspects of the two revolutions of 1917. Neil Harding's *Lenin's Political Thought* demonstrates that Lenin was not an opportunist but on the contrary one of the most doctrinaire leaders in history. The works of A. Rabinowitch, the most accessible being *The Bolsheviks Come to Power*, show that the Bolsheviks were not as monolithic as the Stalinist mythologies claim, and that the October Revolution was more than a coup d'état by a small group of dedicated revolutionaries.

Photographic evidence

Finally a note about photographic evidence. This has to be handled with as much, if not more, care than written evidence. This is perhaps illustrated by the photographs on page 28. They are both from the February Revolution (i.e. March in the modern calendar). The larger photograph is a famous one which has appeared in a number of textbooks with captions like 'A revolutionary patrol in March 1917'. A moment's observation and reflection should, however, put the reader on his or her guard. Firstly, the absurd pose of the soldiers on the mudguards hardly makes driving the vehicle practical. Secondly the man at the back is dressed rather incongruously in workman's jacket but with spats on his feet. As the second photograph shows, this individual also managed to get onto other photographs of the period. None of this totally negates the documentary character of the photographs but it does illustrate the need to treat the visual record with some care.

This is part of the photo on page 43.

A note on dates

Dates are always a problem when dealing with the Russian Revolution. This is because the Tsarist government retained the Julian Calendar (abandoned in most of Europe in the eighteenth century) which was 13 days behind the modern calendar. The Bolshevik Government adopted the modern calendar in March 1918.

In this book all dates are in the modern calendar unless they appear in a document, in which case the original date is retained (followed by the modern one in brackets). The names February and October Revolution are however retained, since these were named by contemporaries before the change of calendar.

A note on the glossary

Words printed in *italic* are contained in the glossary on page 135.

References

1   See D. McLellan, *Karl Marx: His Life and Thought*, p. 457 (Paladin, 1973).
2   For dating see the note above.
3   See E. H. Carr, *The Bolshevik Revolution*, vol. 1, p. 176 (Penguin/Pelican, 1966).
4   J. Wheeler-Bennett, *Brest-Litovsk: The Forgotten Peace* (Macmillan, 1966).
5   An interesting account of this early communism is given in N. Cohn, *The Pursuit of the Millennium* (Paladin, 1970).
6   See his *Prelude to Revolution: The Bolsheviks and the July 1917 Uprising* (Indiana University Press, 1968).
7   L. Trotsky, *The History of the Russian Revolution* (first published in 1930, is available in English in a single volume edition published by Pluto Press in 1977).
8   A. Shlyapnikov, *On the Eve of 1917* (first appeared in 1923, English edition Allison and Busby, 1982). N. Krupskaya, *Memories of Lenin* (first published by Martin Lawrence, republished by Panther and Lawrence Wishart, 1970). F. F. Raskolnikov, *Kronstadt and Petrograd in 1917* (first published in 1925, and in English translation by New Park, New York, 1982). A. F. Ilyin-Zhenevsky (first published in Leningrad in 1929 and in English translation in New York in 1984).
9   David Shub, *Lenin* (New York, 1948, and Pelican, London, 1966).
10 Christopher Hill, *Lenin and the Russian Revolution* (The English University Press, 1947, and Pelican, London, 1971).
11 Marc Ferro, *The Russian Revolution of 1917: The Fall of Tsarism and the Origins of Bolshevik Power* (London, 1972) and *The Bolshevik Revolution: A Social History* (London, 1985).

Bibliography

There are too many books in the English language alone to be able to even select all those of value to the student. The best general histories are still:

E. H. Carr, *The Bolshevik Revolution* (3 volumes, of which volume one is the most important) (Pelican edition, London, 1966)

W. H. Chamberlin, *The Russian Revolution 1917–21* (2 volumes) (Macmillan, 1935), which is very readable and still the best chronological account. It includes some documents in the appendix.

For a wide survey in a few pages there are two new surveys incorporating much recent research:

R. Service, *The Russian Revolution 1900–27* (Macmillan, London, 1986)

B. Williams, *The Russian Revolution 1917–21* (Basil Blackwell, for the Historical Association, Oxford, 1987). This is probably the most accessible introduction to the topic.

Students will also find very useful:

A. Wood, *The Russian Revolution* (Longman Seminar Studies, London, 1979)

Edward Acton, *Rethinking the Russian Revolution* (Edward Arnold, 1990).

There are a number of works on various aspects of the revolution. The following should bring deeper knowledge:

P. Avrich, *Kronstadt 1921* (Princeton, 1970)

J. Bunyan, *Intervention, Civil War and Communism in Russia: April–December 1918* (Oxford, 1936)

J. Bunyan and H. H. Fisher, *The Bolshevik Revolution 1917–18* (Stanford University Press, 1934)

R. V. Daniels, *The Conscience of the Revolution* (Simon and Schuster, New York, 1960) gives details of communist opposition during the revolution

M. Ferro, *The Bolshevik Revolution* (Routledge Kegan Paul, London, 1980) is one of the few attempts at a social history of the revolutions

F. Golder, *Documents in Russian History 1914–17* (Appleton-Century, New York, 1927)

N. Harding, *Lenin's Political Thought*, published in two volumes in 1979 and 1981 and as a combined edition (Macmillan, London, 1983) does for Lenin what David McLellan has done for Marx, i.e. explained their ideas in their own terms. The best book on Lenin yet published

Daniel H. Kaiser (ed.) *The Worker's Revolution in Russia, 1917 – The View from Below* (Cambridge 1987).

G. Leggett, *The Cheka: Lenin's Political Police* (Oxford, 1981)

A. Nove, *An Economic History of the USSR* (Pelican, London, 1989). A classic; now updated, it has useful material on the economic background as well as the revolution itself

A. Rabinowitch, *The Bolsheviks Come to Power* (W. W. Norton & Co., New York, 1976 and New Left Books, London, 1979). Useful for showing the diversity of opinions inside the Bolshevik Party in the final 3 months before the revolution

J. Reed, *Ten Days that Shook the World* (first published in Britain by the Communist Party of GB in 1926, reprinted many times: the Penguin, London, 1977 edition has an interesting introduction by A. J. P. Taylor). A rattling good yarn written by an American eyewitness of the October Revolution

T. H. Rigby, *Lenin's Government: Sovnarkom 1917–22* (Cambridge, 1979)

L. Trotsky, *The History of the Russian Revolution* (Pluto Press, London, 1977). Only deals with the events up to October but is powerfully written. Few leading participants in a historical event can have produced so useful a history. The best account from a Marxist perspective

L. Schapiro, *Origin of the Communist Autocracy* (London, 1955)

L. Schapiro, *1917: The Russian Revolutions and the Origins of Present-Day Communism* (Pelican, London, 1985). The standard conservative history of the revolutions which compares Bolshevism to fascism and denies that they had any meaningful support from the working class

S. A. Smith, *Red Petrograd* (Cambridge, 1983)

J. Wheeler-Bennett, *Brest-Litovsk: The Forgotten Peace* (Macmillan, London, 1983, 1966)

V. I. Lenin's *Collected Works* have appeared in several editions in English, the most complete of them appeared in Moscow (Progress Publishers, 1960–70) in 45 volumes. Lenin's *Selected Works* appeared in three volumes. (Moscow, 1963), revised in 1975. These volumes contain all the main works including:

What is to be done (1902). Lenin's argument for a political leadership of the working class.

One Step Forward, Two Steps Back (1904) on the split with the Mensheviks.

Imperialism – The Highest Stage of Capitalism (1916) on the nature of modern capitalism and the reasons for war in our period of history.

The Tasks of the Proletariat in Our Revolution (The April Theses, 1917) in which he set out the reasons for opposing the Provisional Government.

The State and Revolution (1917) which gave Lenin's interpretation of what the Marxist theory of the state was.

Left-Wing Communism – An Infantile Disorder (1920) in which Lenin attacked the Communist Left in other countries, notably Germany and Holland.

In this book we use the editions published by Lawrence and Wishart Ltd, London.

All these are also published as cheap separate pamphlets by the same publishers.

1 The February Revolution

The collapse of Tsarism

Despite attempts by earlier historians to find some group behind the February Revolution of 1917, it is now generally accepted that it was not planned either by freemasons or Bolsheviks. It was a spontaneous outbreak of an exhausted population. This has led to the emergence of a new view that the February Revolution was neither wanted nor expected by anyone. Whilst this is true in a particular sense, since no one predicted the precise date of the revolution, there is plenty of evidence that both revolutionaries and Tsarist supporters expected some kind of outbreak. Their writings provide a possible catalogue of causes for the collapse of Tsarism.

1.1 Trotsky on the disintegration of the army

The Russian army lost in the whole war more men than any army which ever participated in a national war – approximately two and a half million killed, or 40 per cent of all the losses of the Entente [Russia's alliance with Britain and France]. In the first months the soldiers fell under shell fire unthinkingly or thinking little: but from day to day they gathered experience – bitter experience of the lower ranks who are ignorantly commanded. They measured the confusion of the generals by the number of purposeless manoeuvres on sole-less shoes, the number of dinners not eaten. From the bloody mash of people and things emerged a generalised word, the 'mess', which in the soldiers' jargon was replaced by a still juicier term.

The swiftest of all to disintegrate was the peasant infantry. As a general rule, the artillery with its high percentage of industrial workers, is distinguished by an incomparably greater hospitality to revolutionary ideas: this was clearly evident in 1905. If in 1917, on the contrary, the artillery showed more conservatism than the infantry, the cause lies in the fact that through the infantry divisions, as through a sieve, there passed ever new and less and less trained human masses. The artillery, moreover, suffering infinitely fewer

losses, retained its original cadres. The same thing was observed in   20
other specialised troops. But in the long run the artillery yielded too.
During the retreat from Galicia a secret order was issued by the
commander-in-chief; flog the soldiers for desertion and other crimes.
The soldier Pireiko relates: 'They began to flog soldiers for the most
trivial offences; for example, for a few hours' absence without leave.   25
And sometimes they flogged them in order to rouse their fighting
spirit.' As early as September, 17, 1915, Kuropatkin wrote, citing
Guchkov: 'The lower orders began the war with enthusiasm; but now
they are weary, and with the continual retreats have lost faith in a
victory.'   30

L. Trotsky, *The History of the Russian Revolution*, 1932, 1977, 1980

Questions

1   What three 'bitter experiences' could Russian soldiers have assimi-
     lated during the war? What impact do you think these experiences
     might have had?
2   How does the author account for the contrasting political attitudes of
     the infantry and artillery to the war?
3   What attitude do (i) the author and (ii) Kuropatkin have towards the
     ordinary soldiers? Why do they hold such attitudes?
4   If the peasantry was more demoralised by the war, why did revolu-
     tion first break out in the towns?

1.2   The President of the Duma on the war effort

The War Department was particularly weak in first aid. Though it
had neither carts, horses, nor first aid material, . . . it allowed no
other organization on the field. There seemed no other course than to
bring the state of affairs to the attention of Grand Duke Nicholas
Nicholaevich [uncle of the Tsar]. I wrote him a letter in which I told   5
him that patriotic enthusiasm had called forth a number of volunteer
sanitary organizations, but that they could do nothing because of
Evdokimov, the head of the sanitary division of the Ministry of War
. . . I also went to see the old Empress, Marie Fedorovna, who lived
on Elagin Island. When I told her the situation she was horrified.   10
'Tell me, what should be done?', asked the Empress.
    I advised her to send a telegram to Nicholas Nicholaevich urging
him to command Evdokimov to put things in order and to allow the

Red Cross to go to work. She asked me to write such a telegram in
her name.   15
  As a result of these efforts there came a telegram, followed by a
letter, from the Grand Duke stating that he agreed with the president
of the Duma, and that he would take the necessary measures. Soon
after that Evdokimov was called to Headquarters. A little later Prince
Alexander Petrovich of Oldenburg was made the head of the sanitary- 20
evacuation division with dictatorial powers. Grand Duke Nicholas
wrote me that he had long before insisted on the removal of
Evdokimov, but that it could not be done because he had the
protection of Sukhomlinov and the Empress Alexandra Fedorovna. It
was said that the young Empress persuaded the Emperor to leave   25
Evdokimov in his place in order to spite the old Empress ...
  Soon after my arrival at Warsaw in November (O.S.) 1914, I had a
call from Vyrubov (V.V.), a representative of the Zemstvo Union,
who asked me to go with him to the Warsaw–Vienna station where
there were about eighteen thousand men, wounded in the battles near 30
Lodz and Berezina. There I saw a frightful scene. On the floor,
without even a bedding of straw, in mud and slush, lay innumerable
wounded, whose pitiful groans and cries filled the air. 'For God's
sake, get them to attend us. No one has looked after our wounds for
five days.'   35

**M. V. Rodzianko, 'Arkhiv Russkoi Revolutsii' in F. A. Golder, *Docu-
ments of Russian History 1914–17*, 1964**

**1.3 The paralysis of the Tsar's government. The President of the
Duma reports his conversation with the Commander-in-Chief of
the Russian Army, the Grand Duke Nicholas (uncle of the Tsar) in
November 1914.**

The Grand Duke stated that he was obliged to stop fighting, temporarily, for lack of ammunition and boots.
  'You have influence,' he said. 'You are trusted. Try and get boots
for the army, as soon as possible.'
  I replied that this could be done if the *zemstvos* and public   5
organizations were asked to help. There was plenty of material and
labor in Russia. But as it stood then, one guberniia [district] had
leather, another nails, another soles, and still another cheap labor.

The best thing to do would be to call a congress of the heads of the guberniia zemstvos and ask their cooperation. The Grand Duke was greatly pleased with this idea.   10

When I returned to Petrograd, I asked members of the Duma their opinion as to the best way to get boots. After considering the matter, we decided to circularize heads of zemstvos and mayors of cities. In a short time, we received very encouraging replies. Realizing that there   15 might be objections from the Government to calling a congress, I decided to talk it over separately with some of the Ministers. Krivoshein, Sukhomlinov, and Goremykin liked the idea and promised to support it when it came up in the Council of Ministers. My interview with Minister Maklakov was quite out of the ordinary. When I   20 explained that it was the wish of the Commander-in-Chief to secure a supply of boots for the army quickly through the help of the zemstvos, and for that purpose there would be a meeting of the heads of the cities and zemstvos, Maklakov said: 'Yes, yes; what you tell me agrees perfectly with the information I get from my agents.'   25

'What information?'

'According to the information of my agents, the congress to take up the needs of the army has for its real object to discuss political questions and demand a constitution.'

M. V. Rodzianko, 'Arkhiv Russkoi Revolutsii' in F. A. Golder, *Documents of Russian History 1914–17*, 1964

Questions

1   What indications are there in **1.2** and **1.3** that Nicholas II's government had made few war preparations? What does this tell you about the Russian Government?
2   What does the evidence of Rodzianko reveal about the Russian Royal Family? How can you account for this?
3   Explain the motives of the various Tsarist officials in rejecting the help of the voluntary organisations?
4   Rodzianko's *Memoirs* and Trotsky's *The History of the Russian Revolution* were written at about the same time. From these extracts, which appears to be the most useful to historians as evidence? Explain how you reached your choice.
5   'The First World War was the only reason for the fall of the Tsar.' Discuss.

It was not only the troops who were facing an increasingly impossible position. On the home front in both cities and villages the war strained the fragile economic infrastructure to the limit. For workers in the towns, 'real wages fell during the war – very slowly during 1914 and 1915, and then increasingly rapidly as 1916 wore on. The crucial importance of defence industries in the capital meant that Petrograd was probably the only area in Russia where overall real wages rose until the winter of 1916. Thereafter, however, real wages began to fall rapidly, and by the time of the February Revolution they were probably 15% to 20% below the level of 1913' (S. A. Smith, *Red Petrograd*, 1985, p. 46). On top of declining wages came the breakdown of the transport system. Much of the railway rolling stock was committed to troop movements and this aggravated food shortages in the northern cities.

1.4   Bolshevik reports on the food crisis in 1916

In Bryansk county, Orel province, there is no rye flour, salt, paraffin or sugar. In Bryansk a pound of sugar costs from one to one ruble fifty. Discontent is rife and more than once there have been strikes in the factories and plants with the demand for 'flour and sugar'. There is in Bryansk county a village called Star, where there is in the village 5 a factory making glass products which belong to the Maltsov company and is engaged in war contracts. Workers there struck on 8 October (1916) because they had not eaten bread for two weeks, having only potatoes: they selected two spokesmen and sent them to the factory manager with a demand for flour and sugar (for the 10 company had undertaken to procure the items at pre-war prices as it kept wages at peacetime levels). The manager could not give an answer but just made promises. The following day the two spokesmen were arrested as unreliable elements and held under emergency regulations; two days later the workers went back but still did not get 15 the bread. There is no organisation at the factory . . .

From 13 to 16 November I stayed in the town of Zhizdra, Kaluga province. There was an acute shortage of domestic items; at all times there was no flour, sugar or paraffin at all. No commodities other than hay were being brought in from the villages. I then travelled 20 round the villages: grumbling, discontent and a vague apprehension all around.

From Alexander Shlyapnikov, *On the Eve of 1917*, 1982

1.5   The number of strikes in Petrograd 1914–17

Month	Political Strikes			Economic Strikes		
	No. of strikes	No. of strikers	No. of working days lost through strikes	No. of strikes	No. of strikers	No. of working days lost through strikes
1914						
July 1–18	–	160,099	–	–	580	–
July 19	26	27,400	48,540	16	10,942	76,914
August	–	–	–	–	–	–
September	1	1,400	280	3	905	1,180
October	–	–	–	2	160	42
November	2	3,150	1,260	3	785	785
December	–	–	–	2	1,020	1,240
1915						
January	14	2,595	2,488.5	2	115	565
February	6	340	183.5	2	120	85
March	–	–	–	6	461	311
April	–	–	–	7	4,064	9,988
May	10	1,259	899	7	2,571	1,607
June	–	–	–	9	1,141	531
July	–	–	–	29	17,934	33,965.5
August	24	23,178	24,574.5	16	11,640	15,879
September	70	82,728	176,623.5	13	7,470	12,730.5
October	10	11,268	34,911.5	21	13,350	69,031.5
November	5	11,020	6,280	19	6,838	7,509.5
December	7	8,985	5,624.5	26	13,284	15,261
1916						
January	68	61,447	64,566	35	16,418	37,749.5
February	3	3,200	170	55	53,723	220,026.5
March	51	77,877	386,405.5	16	11,811	81,162.5
April	7	14,152	87,019	48	25,112	47,758
May	3	8,932	2,282	42	26,756	125,496
June	6	3,452	3,062.5	37	15,603	72,191.5
July	2	5,333	60,025	27	20,326	26,004
August	4	1,686	2,761	18	6,259	10,934.5
September	2	2,800	2,400	33	24,918	84,783.5
October	177	174,592	452,158.5	12	15,184	12,912
November	6	22,950	8,283	24	18,592	30,204.5
December	1	1,000	25	7	8,798	29,835
1917						
January	135	151,886	144,116	34	24,869	59,024.5
Feb. 1–17	85	123,953	137,508	14	19,809	62,647
TOTAL	1,044	826,593	1,652,446.5	585	380,978	1,148,354

I. P. Leiberov, 'Stachechnaya bor'ba petrogradskogo proletariata v period pervoi mirovoi voiny (19 iyulya 1914g.–16 fevralya 1917g.)', *Istoriya rabochego klassa Leningrada*, issue 2 (Leningrad, 1963), pp. 166, 177, 183.

Questions

1   What, according to Shlyapnikov [**1.4**], was the basic cause of strikes
    at this time?
2   What effect did the declaration of war have on the level of strikes
    [**1.5**]? What does this suggest about the attitudes of the workers at
    this time?
3   How far do the statistics [**1.5**] confirm the picture painted by
    Shlyapnikov [**1.4**]?
4   Draw a line graph of the total number of strikes throughout the war.
    What conclusions does this enable you to reach about the attitudes of
    the workers during the war?
5   Does Shlyapnikov's evidence [**1.4**] confirm or deny the view that the
    February Revolution was a spontaneous, unorganised uprising? In
    what ways does it do so?

Despite the immense problems which the war brought to Russia, the
Tsar, earnestly reinforced by his wife, the Tsarina Alexandra, refused
all reasonable advice from those who were most concerned that Russia
remained a monarchy. Even the murder of the favourite, Rasputin, by
members of the Royal Family, together with the fanatically monarchist
Duma Deputy, Purishkevich, did not alter the headlong course to
destruction of the Russian Monarchy.

1.6   Letters of the Empress to her husband

Sept. 20, 27, 1915
... Gregory begs you earnestly to name Protopopov there [Ministry
of the Interior]. You know him and had such a good impression of
him – happens to be of the Duma (is not left) and so will know how
to be with them ... God bless yr. new choice of Protopopov – our   5
Friend says you have done a very wise act in naming him.

Nov. 28, 1915
... Now, before I forget, I must give you over a message from our
Friend, prompted by what He saw in the night. He begs you to order
that one should advance near Riga, says it is necessary, otherwise the   10
Germans will settle down so firmly through all the winter, that it will
cost endless bloodshed and trouble to make them move ...

June 17, 1916
... He [Rasputin] begs we should not yet strongly advance in the
north because he says, if our successes continue being good in the   15
south, they will themselves retreat from the north ...

Nov. 24, 1916

I entreat you dont go and change Protopopov now, he will be alright, give him the chance to get the food supply matter into his hands and I assure you, all will go well ... Of course I more than regret that   20
Trepov [Minister of Transport] is at the head ... Protopopov is honestly for us ... Protopopov venerates our Friend and will be blessed ... dont change Protopopov ...

Dec. 6, 1916

... Once you have said that you want to keep Protopopov, how does   25
he [Prime Minister Trepov] go against you? Bring down your fist on the table. Don't yield. Be the boss. Obey your firm little wife and our Friend. Believe in us.

From F. A. Golder, *Documents of Russian History* 1914–17, 1964. The Tsarina wrote in English. The punctuation and grammar has not been altered from the original.

Questions

1   Over what areas of government decision-making did Rasputin have influence? Assess what his impact on the effectiveness of government must have been.
2   On what basis did the Tsarina judge whether a minister should be appointed or dismissed? What effects do you think this had on government?
3   What evidence do these letters give of (i) Rasputin's special position in relation to the Empress and (ii) the Tsarina's view of her husband?
4   Compare the strengths and weaknesses of these letters as evidence for historians with both the extracts from Trotsky's history [1.1] and Rodzianko's memoirs [1.2 and 1.3].

1.7   2 December 1916. A patriotic declaration in the Duma by the leader of the *Black Hundreds*.

Gentlemen, I mount this tribune today with inexpressible emotion, and this, not because I have left the ranks of my party. It is impossible for me to abandon the ranks of the Right, for I am the most extreme of the Rights. But there are moments when one cannot speak from the belfry of a district or provincial town, but must ring   5
the alarm from the bell tower of Ivan the Great ...

Russia has reached the end of her patience waiting for a strong
government – not the authority of police bigotry, such as Russia has
known since olden times – but a Government that could show us it
has some programme and some system. But the only strong authority   10
which we see is the systematic and consistent internal disorganisation
of the State. (Cries on the left: 'Right!') The disorganisation of our
rear is undoubtedly being carried out by a strong and relentless hand.
This system was set up by William himself and is being thoroughly
practised with the aid of the German party working in our rear, and   15
of those elements – the scum of Russian society – who can bring
themselves to serve the enemy . . .

Gentlemen, we must plead with the Sovereign, and you, his loyal
servants, chosen to do his bidding, you, who bear the brunt of
responsibility for the course of the Russian ship of state, in common   20
with us, go to Headquarters and plead with the Sovereign . . . to
deliver Russia from Rasputin . . .

**V. V. Purishkevich, 'Comment j'ai tué Raspoutine' from F. A.
Golder, *Documents of Russian History 1914–17*, 1964**

1.8   A Palace revolution?

The idea that it was necessary to force the Tsar to abdicate seemed to
take hold of Petrograd at the end of 1916, and the beginning of 1917.
A number of people from the higher circles declared that the Duma
and its president should undertake this task and save the army and
Russia.   5

On January 21 (1917), there came to see me, quite unexpectedly,
Grand Duke Michael Alexandrovitch (brother of the Tsar), who said
'I should like to talk to you about what is going on and to consult
you as to what should be done. We understand the situation . . . Do
you think there is going to be a revolution?   10

'As long as the war goes on, the people realise that division means
ruin for the army. But there is another kind of danger. The Government and the Empress lead Russia toward a separate peace, to shame
and into the arms of Germany . . . There is still time to save Russia
. . . I am sorry to say, however, that this could be done only if the   15
Empress were removed . . . As long as she is in power we shall drift
towards ruin.'

**From Rodzianko's Memoirs cited in F. A. Golder, *Documents of
Russian History 1914–17*, 1964**

1.9

The cartoon shown here was found in the files of the Okhrana after the February Revolution

Questions

1 Purishkevich declared that he was 'of the Right' [**1.7, line 3**]. In Russia in 1916 what did this suggest he believed in?

2 Who is the 'William' referred to in Purishkevich's speech [**1.7, line 14**]? Who does Purishkevich think is leading the 'German party working in our rear' [**1.7, line 15**]? Assess the impact of the 'German party' on the war effort.

3 Examine the differences and similarities in the reasons given for Russia's ills in the accounts of Rodzianko and Purishkevich. Why do they pick on different scapegoats?

4 Which of the two accounts is (i) more reliable and (ii) more revealing to historians? Justify your response.

5 Was the Russian monarchy saveable by the end of 1916?

6 Compare cartoon 1.9 with the Tsarina's letters. How accurate is it in its portrayal of the relationship between Rasputin and the Romanov family?

From riot to revolution

Whilst the schemes for a 'palace revolution' remained the talk of the
salons of the wealthy, events were already beginning to take a different
course. Time had run out for the Russian monarchy. On International
Women's Day, 8 March (Feb 23rd under the old calendar) the usual
socialist holiday took place. There were the usual demonstrations and
token strikes. However, the next day the workers refused to return to
work and women textile workers took the lead in marching on the Town
Hall to demand bread. Within a few hours Petrograd was gripped by a
massive general strike. Regiment after regiment of the 160,000 strong
garrison in the capital went over to the workers and began to join in
attacks on the police. The bread riots had become the much-feared
revolution. The Empress tried to reassure the Emperor that this was
simply: '. . . a hooligan movement. All will calm down if only the Duma
will behave itself.' Virtually the Tsar's last act was to order the suspen-
sion of the Duma. This reduced it to a state of near paralysis at the very
time when a revolutionary crowd was advancing on the Duma singing
the Marseillaise, and expecting the Duma to become the head of a
revolution the Duma deputies did not want.

A monarchist Duma Deputy described what followed.

1.10   The paralysis of the old Duma in March 1917

Rodzianko [see Key Personalities] explained the situation and asked
'What should be done?' . . .

What? I do not know. Someone, it seems proposed that the Duma
should declare itself as the Government . . . declare that it will not
disperse . . . will not obey the order . . . declare itself a Constituent   5
Assembly. This proposition did not receive, could not receive, support . . . Someone demanded that the Duma should say whether it is
with the old Government or with the people, the very people now on
the way, and to whom an answer must be given . . .

Kerensky alone, accustomed to such things, knew how to dance on   10
the revolutionary bog . . . and he grew with each minute . . . This
explains why during the first period of the revolution (without taking
into consideration his personal qualities, for he was a first–class actor)
Kerensky played such a prominent part. There were people who
listened to him . . . Perhaps it would be better to say that there were   15
armed people who listened to him. In time of revolution only those
who have guns count . . .

The opposing side was not asleep. Throughout the city in every barrack and every factory, elections were going on ... One for every thousand ... for the workers and soldiers deputies ... the mass 'organised', in other words it was organised so that it could be used.

And we? We had a very poor idea of what was going on.

From the memories of V. V. Shulgin in F. A. Golder, *Documents of Russian History 1914–17*, 1964

1.11 A 'Faraon' (pharaoh) is arrested by the revolutionary crowd. 'Pharaoh' was the popular nickname for the police. The old Tsarist police force had the most to lose from the revolution and carried on fighting, often sniping from rooftops at the demonstrations.

In M. Lyons, *Russia in Original Photographs*, 1977.

Questions

1 How does photograph 1.11 confirm or deny the view given in the written sources in this chapter?

2 What elements does the picture contain to reveal some of the motive forces of the revolution?

3   What evidence is there to show who took or who possessed the picture?

4   Compare photograph **1.11** with those on p. 28. Are there any features which would lead you to question its authenticity?

1.12   The Tsar describes his abdication

15 March, Thursday

In the morning Ruzski came and read his very long direct-wire talk with Rodzianko. According to this, the situation in Petrograd is such that a Ministry of the Duma would now be powerless to do anything, for it has to contend with the Social Democratic Party, represented   5
by the workers committee. My abdication is required. Ruszki transmitted this talk to Headquarters, and Alexeyev sent it on to all the commanders-in-chief. By 2 o'clock replies were received from them. The gist of them is that in order to save Russia and keep the army at the front quiet, such a step must be taken. I have agreed. From   10
Headquarters has been sent the draft of a manifesto. In the evening Guchkov and Shulgin arrived from Petrograd, with whom I discussed the matter, and I handed them the signed and altered manifesto. At 1 o'clock in the morning (16th) I left Pskov, with a heavy heart because of the things gone through. All around me there is treachery,   15
cowardice and deceit.

From the diary of Nicholas II in F. A. Golder, *Documents of Russian History 1914–17,* **1964**

Questions

1   What was a 'Constituent Assembly' [**1.10, lines 5–6**]? Why did the Duma deputies refuse, at this stage, to support a Constituent Assembly?

2   What was the source of Kerensky's influence at this early stage of the revolution [**1.10**]?

3   How do **1.10** and **1.11** show why the Duma was not really in a position to lead the revolution?

4   In the Tsar's diary what does he mean when he refers to 'the workers committee' [**1.12, line 6**], and what was the Social Democratic Party [**1.12, line 5**]?

5   What indications are there in the Tsar's letters that the troops at the front shared some of the attitudes of the Petrograd garrison?

6   What was the Tsar's view of the causes of his abdication? From the
      evidence in all the documents in this chapter what are the other
      possible causes?
7   Who did Shulgin mean by the 'opposing side' [**1.10, line 18**]? What
      evidence is there that he did not believe the February Revolution to
      be a spontaneous affair? Why do you think he held this opinion?

Having obtained the abdication of the Tsar, the Duma politicians, led by
the ex-president of the Duma, Rodzianko, and the leader of the Constitutional Democrats (Kadets), Milyukov, still hoped to 'save the dynasty'.
Thus they loyally dissolved the Duma in compliance with the last decree
of Nicholas II. However, to try to take a lead over the popular movement
they moved to another room of the Tauride Palace and set up a
'temporary committee' of the Duma. This temporary committee was to
form the basis of the 'Provisional Government' that nominally ran Russia
until the Bolsheviks assumed power on 7 November 1917. On the same
day as the Provisional Government came into existence, the Petrograd
Soviet, which had flourished briefly in 1905, was reconvened, at
Menshevik instigation. Thus began the system known as 'dual power'.

1.13   The re-formation of the Petrograd Soviet on 12 March 1917, described by a Menshevik Internationalist

Standing on stools, their rifles in their hands, agitated and stuttering,
straining all their powers to give a connected account of the messages
entrusted to them, with their thoughts concentrated on the narrative
itself, in unaccustomed and half-fantastic surroundings, without
thinking and perhaps quite unaware of the whole significance of the   5
facts they were reporting, in simple rugged language that infinitely
strengthened the effect of the absence of emphasis – one after another
the soldiers' delegates told of what had been happening in their
companies. Their stories were artless, and repeated each other almost
word for word. The audience listened as children listen to a wonder-   10
ful, enthralling fairy-tale they know by heart, holding their breaths,
with craning necks and unseeing eyes.
  'We're from the Volhynian Regiment . . . the Pavlovsky . . . the
Lithuanian . . . the Cuxholm . . . the Sappers . . . the Chasseurs . . .
the Finnish . . . the Grenadiers . . .' The name of each of the magnifi-   15
cent regiments that had launched the revolution was met with a
storm of applause.

'We had a meeting . . .' 'We have been told to say . . .' 'The
officers hid . . .' 'To join the Soviet of Workers' Deputies . . .' 'They
told us to say that we refuse to serve against the people any more,   20
we're going to join with our brother-workers, all united, to defend
the people's cause . . . We would lay down our lives for that.' 'Our
general meeting told us to greet you . . .' 'Long live the revolution!'
the delegate would add in a voice already extinguished by the throb-
bing roar of the meeting . . .   25

It was then and there proposed, and approved with storms of
applause – to fuse together the revolutionary army and the proletariat
of the capital and create a united organisation to be called from then
on the 'Soviet of Workers' and Soldiers' Deputies . . .'

N. N. Sukhanov, *The Russian Revolution 1917. A Personal Memoir*,
translated and edited by Joel Carmichael, 1955

1.14   Soviet Order No. 1 (15 March 1917)

To the garrison of the Petrograd Military District, to all soldiers of
the guard, army, artillery and fleet for immediate and exact execution,
and to all workers of Petrograd for their information.

The Soviet of Workers' and Soldiers' Deputies has decreed:

1   Committees are to be elected immediately in all companies,   5
    battalions, regiments, parks, batteries, squadrons, and individual
    units of the different forms of military directorates, and in all
    naval vessels, from the elected representatives of the rank and file
    of the above-mentioned units.

2   All troop units which have not yet elected their representatives to   10
    the Soviet of Workers' Deputies are to elect one representative
    per company. Such representatives are to appear, with written
    confirmation, at the State Duma building at 10 a.m. on 2 March.

3   In all political actions, troop units are subordinate to the Soviet of
    Workers' and Soldiers' Deputies and to the committees thereof.   15

4   The orders of the Military Commission of the State Duma are to
    be obeyed, with the exception of those instances in which they
    contradict the orders and decrees of the Soviet of Workers' and
    Soldiers' Deputies.

5   All types of arms, such as rifles, machine guns, armoured cars and   20
    others, must be put at the disposal of company and battalion
    committees and under their control, and are not, in any case, to
    be issued to officers, even upon demand.

6 On duty and in the performance of service responsibilities, soldiers must observe the strictest military discipline, but when off   25
   duty, in their political, civil and private lives, soldiers shall enjoy
   fully and completely the same rights as all citizens. In particular,
   standing at attention and compulsory saluting when off-duty are
   abolished.

7 In the same way, addressing officers by honorary titles ('Your   30
   Excellency', 'Your Honour' etc) is abolished and is replaced by
   the following form of address: 'Mr General', 'Mr Colonel' etc.
      Addressing soldiers rudely by anyone of higher rank and in
   particular addressing soldiers by 'ty' (thou) is prohibited and any
   breach of this provision, as well as any misunderstandings   35
   between officers and soldiers, are to be reported by the latter to
   the company committees.

Petrograd Soviet of Soldiers' and Workers' Deputies

'Izvestia' (15 March 1917) from M. McCauley, *The Russian Revolution
and the Soviet State 1917–21*, 1975

Questions

1 What did Sukhanov mean when he said that the soldiers reports to
   the Soviet were 'artless' [**1.13, line 9**]?

2 How accurate was Sukhanov's assertion that the 'regiments . . . had
   launched the revolution' [**1.13, line 16**]?

3 Compare Sukhanov's account with that of Shulgin [**1.10**]. What
   evidence does Sukhanov's account give which (i) reveals a different
   attitude to ordinary working people and (ii) contradicts Shulgin's
   view of the organisation of the revolution?

4 In what important respects do **1.13** and **1.14** confirm Shulgin's thinking about the revolution, and how?

5 Compare **1.13** and **1.14**. Comment on their value as evidence for
   historians of the Russian revolution in relation to:
   (i) their respective degrees of reliability
   (ii) the importance of the information they contain
   (iii) their interest as reading material

6 'In March 1917 the Petrograd Soviet exercised state power but it
   would not recognise this fact.' Comment on the validity of this
   statement.

2 Problems of the Provisional Government

The conduct of war: conflict and crisis

The expectations aroused by the fall of the Tsar created enormous problems for the Provisional Government. Russia had become, as Lenin himself noted, the country in the world with the greatest freedom. Political prisoners were released, press censorship ended, the Tsar's secret police (the Okhrana) was disbanded, and the death penalty was abolished. However, the bread shortage did not end with the fall of the Tsar. Peasants now hoped for a fairer distribution of land, and workers began to take over the factories. Above all, there was an almost universal desire for peace.

This placed the Provisional Government in a difficult position. It would only be 'provisional' until a Constituent Assembly was called. But most of its members were agreed that the Constituent Assembly should wait until after the war. This dubious legal basis for the Provisional Government only emphasised the fact that the real power lay with the Petrograd Soviet. As the Minister of War, Guchkov, lamented, the Provisional Government could not so much as send a telegram without the permission of the Soviet. The Soviet in its turn was dominated by socialist parties like the Mensheviks and the Socialist Revolutionaries (SRs). However, both the Mensheviks and SRs thought it would be premature for a socialist party to rule, and expected the bourgeois parties of the Provisional Government to govern Russia but without carrying out any policies hostile to 'the revolutionary democracy'. The contradictions in this policy were soon apparent over the effect 'Soviet Order No. 1' had on the conduct of the war, as a British officer later recorded.

2.1 The condition of the Russian Army. The British Military Attaché reports to the British Ambassador in Petrograd in April 1917

I returned to Petrograd from a visit to the Northern front on April 28. I gave you my opinion of the deplorable state of things at the front. Units have been turned into political debating societies; the

infantry refuses to allow the guns to shoot at the enemy; parleying in
betrayal of the Allies and the best interests of Russia takes place daily   5
with the enemy who laughs at the credulity of the Russian peasant-
soldier. Many senior officers complained that the Government, to
which every army has a right to look for support, has left all the
burden of dealing with the agitation to the army. In Petrograd things
are growing worse daily. The tens of thousands of able-bodied men   10
in uniform who saunter about the streets without a thought of going
to the front or working to prepare themselves for the war, when every
able-bodied man and most of the women in England and France are
straining every nerve to beat the common enemy, will be a disgrace
for all time for the Russian people and its Government.   15

Major-General Sir Alfred Knox, *With the Russian Army 1914–17,* 1921

2.2

'*At last I have found the ideal soldier who will keep
quiet and carry out orders without arguing.*'

**Cartoon from *Golos Truda* (Petrograd, 27 October 1917) by Robert
Minor, from the Hoover Institution Library (originally published in
'The Masses' (New York), July 1916**

Questions

1   Using **2.1** explain why the thoughts of the common soldier were turning towards home after February 1917.
2   How does this document help us to understand more clearly the importance of an official document like 'Soviet Order No. 1' [see **1.14**]?
3   'Soviet Order No. 1' [**1.14**] was described by Trotsky as 'the only respectable one to come out of the February (March) Revolution' and by the Supreme Commander of the Army, General Alexeyev, as 'the last nail in the coffin of our army'. How do you account for these diametrically opposed views?
4   Who is General Knox thinking of when he talks of 'the army' in **2.1 line 9**? How far does this limit the value of his evidence?
5   What can we tell about the likely readership of *Golos Truda* from the cartoon [**2.2**]?
6   How accurate a comment is **2.2** on the views expressed in **2.1**?

The first Provisional Government was led by Prince George Lvov, well known as the head of the zemstvo union which had tried to organise support for the war effort. It was made up of the representatives of the industrial bourgeoisie and professional classes. Most of the ten ministers in the first Provisional Government could be described as liberals and nearly all were connected by freemasonry ties. Half the ministers were from the Kadet Party which was led by the Minister of Foreign Affairs, P. N. Milyukov. However, this did not help the unity of the Provisional Government as Milyukov had moved further to the right since the Party was founded in 1905. Whilst he favoured a constitutional monarchy, most of his fellow-Kadets were republicans and wanted to co-operate with the Soviet.

It was on the issue of the war that Milyukov provoked the first crisis of the regime. Here he lined up alongside the *Octobrist* Minister of War, A. I. Guchkov. Both men wished to continue the war policy of the Tsar, fighting alongside the Entente powers, Britain and France. This was to cause immediate conflict with the Soviet since all the parties represented in it regarded the war as the product of imperialist policy. The Soviet Executive hoped to get a negotiated peace as quickly as possible and spent a great deal of time debating possible peace terms. The gulf between Milyukov and the Soviets reached crisis point in May 1917 when Milyukov's Note to the Allies was published. This led to two days of demonstrations (3 and 4 May) against the war and to the resignation of Milyukov and Guchkov.

2.3   An outline of the policy of the Entente Powers by the British Ambassador in March 1917

Our only possible policy was to strengthen the hands of the Provisional Government in their struggle with the Soviet. The latter was ruining the army with its socialist propaganda, and though the majority of its members professed themselves in favour of continuing the war, those on the extreme Left advocated peace at any price. The   5
speedy recognition of the Provisional Government was, therefore, in my opinion, necessary; but when, on March 18, Milyukov broached the subject to me, I told him that before acting on the authorisation already given me, I must have the assurance that the new Government was prepared to fight the war out to a finish and to restore   10
discipline in the army. Milyukov gave me this assurance, but said that they were obliged to proceed cautiously on account of the extremists, and that his own position was a difficult one. He was regarded with suspicion for having supported the Grand Duke Michael's [Tsar Nicholas II's brother] claim to the throne and he   15
must either make some concessions or resign. Which course, he asked, would I prefer him to take? The former, I unhesitatingly replied.

Sir George Buchanan, *My Mission to Russia*, vol. II, 1923

2.4   The Petrograd Soviet's Appeal to the Peoples of the World (28 March 1917)

Comrade-proletarians and toilers of all countries:
    We, Russian workers and soldiers, united in the Petrograd Soviet of Workers' and Soldiers' Deputies, send you the warmest greetings and announce the great event. The Russian democracy has shattered in the dust the age-long despotism of the Tsar and enters your family 5
(of nations) as an equal, and as a mighty force in the struggle for our common liberation ... Long live the international solidarity of the proletariat, and its struggle for final victory!
    ... We are appealing to our brother-proletarians of the Austro-German coalition, and, first of all, to the German proletariat. From   10
the first days of the war, you were assured that by raising arms against autocratic Russia you were defending the culture of Europe from Asiatic despotism. Many of you saw in this a justification of that support which you were giving to the war. Now this justification is gone: democratic Russia cannot be a threat to liberty and civilisation. 15

We will firmly defend our own liberty from all reactionary
attempts from within, as well as from without. The Russian revolution will not retreat before the bayonets of conquerors, and will not
allow itself to be crushed by foreign military force. But we are calling
to you: Throw off the yoke of semi-autocratic rule, as the Russian   20
people have shaken off the Tsar's autocracy; refuse to serve as an
instrument of conquest and violence in the hands of kings, land-
owners and bankers – and then by our united efforts, we will stop the
horrible butchery ...

Toilers of all countries: We hold out to you the hand of brother-   25
hood across the mountains of our brothers' corpses, across rivers of
innocent blood and tears ... we appeal to you for the re-establishment and strengthening of international unity. In it is the pledge of
our future victories and the complete liberation of humanity.

Proletarians of all countries, unite!   30

Petrograd Soviet of Workers' and Soldiers' Deputies

From F. A. Golder, *Documents of Russian History 1914–17*, 1964

2.5   Bolshevik Resolution on the War proposed by Lenin (12 May 1917)

No trust can be placed in the present government's promises to
renounce annexations, i.e. conquests of foreign countries or retention
by force of any nationality within the confines of Russia. For, in the
first place, the capitalists, bound together by the thousand threads of
banking capital, cannot renounce annexations in this war without   5
renouncing the profits from the thousands of millions invested in
loans, concessions, war industries etc. And secondly, the new government, after renouncing annexations to mislead the people, declared
through Milyukov (Moscow, April 9th, 1917) that it had no intention
of renouncing them ... Therefore, in warning the people against the   10
capitalist's empty promises, the Conference declares that it is necessary to make a clear distinction between a renunciation of annexations
in word and a renunciation of annexations in deed, i.e. the immediate
publication and abrogation of all the secret, predatory treaties and the
immediate granting to all nationalities of the right to determine by   15
free voting whether they wish to be independent states or to be part
of another state ...

In regard to the most important question of all, namely how to end
the present capitalist war as soon as possible, not by a coercive peace,
but by a truly democratic peace, the Conference recognises and   20
declares the following:

This war cannot be ended by a refusal of the soldiers of one side
only to continue the war, by a simple cessation of hostilities by one of
the belligerents.

The Conference reiterates its protest against the base slander   25
spread by the capitalists against our Party to the effect that we are in
favour of a separate peace with Germany. We consider the German
capitalists to be as predatory as the Russian, British, French, and
other capitalists, and Emperor Wilhelm as bad a crowned brigand as
Nicholas II or the British, Italian, Rumanian and all other monarchs.   30

Our Party will patiently but persistently explain to the people the
truth that wars are waged by GOVERNMENTS, that wars are
always indissolubly bound up with the policies of definite CLASSES,
that this war can be terminated by a democratic peace ONLY if the
entire state power, in at least several of the belligerent countries, has   35
passed to the class of the proletarians and semi-proletarians which is
really capable of putting an end to the oppressive rule of capital ...

**'Resolution on the War' passed at the 7th All-Russia Conference of
the Russian Social Democratic Labour Party (Bolshevik). This translation is taken from V. I. Lenin, *Selected Works*, vol. 2, 1977 edition.**

2.6   Milyukov's Note of 1 May 1917 on the war aims of the Provisional Government

On April 9 of the present year, the Provisional Government issued a
declaration to the citizens, containing the views of the Government of
free Russia regarding the aims of the present war. The Minister of
Foreign Affairs has instructed me to communicate to you the contents
of the document referred to, and to make at the same time the   5
following comments:

Our enemies have been striving of late to sow discord among the
Allies, disseminating absurd reports alleging that Russia is ready to
conclude a separate peace with the Central Powers. The text of the
attached document will most effectively refute such falsehoods. You   10
will note from the same that the general principles enunciated by the
Provisional Government are in entire agreement with those lofty ideas
which have been constantly expressed, up to the very last moment,

by many eminent statesmen in the Allied countries, and which were
given especially vivid expression in the declaration of the president of   15
our new Ally, the great republic across the Atlantic.

The Government under the old regime was, of course, incapable of
grasping and sharing these ideas of the liberating character of the
war, the establishment of a firm basis for the amicable existence of
the nations, of self-determination for oppressed peoples, and so forth.   20
Emancipated Russia, however, can now speak in a language that will
be comprehensible to the leading democracies of our own time, and
she now hastens to add her voice to those of her Allies. Imbued with
the new spirit of a free democracy, the declaration of the Provisional
Government cannot, of course, afford the least excuse for the   25
assumption that the revolution has entailed any slackening on the part
of Russia in the common struggle of the Allies. Quite to the contrary,
the aspiration of the entire nation to carry the world war to a decisive
victory has grown more powerful, thanks to our understanding of our
common responsibility, shared by each and every one. This striving   30
has become still more active, since it is concentrated on a task which
touches all and is urgent – the task of driving out the enemy who has
invaded our country. It is obvious, as stated in the communicated
document, that the Provisional Government, while safeguarding the
rights of our own country, will, in every way, observe the obligations   35
assumed towards our Allies.

**From the Kadet newspaper *Rech* (Speech) 3.5.1917. Translated in
F. A. Golder, *Documents of Russian History 1914–17*, 1964**

Questions

1   Analyse **2.3** to **2.6**. For each document state, with supporting
    evidence:
    (i) who the document's intended audience was
    (ii) its attitude to the further development of the revolution and/or
         war
    (iii) its proposals for ending the war
2   In the light of the evidence in **2.1**, assess how successful the various
    policies in **2.3** to **2.6** were likely to be.
3   'Pacifist', 'imperialist', 'defeatist', 'nationalist', and 'defencist' were
    only some of the attacks made on each of the positions held by the
    various parties in the Russian revolutionary year. Test your under-
    standing of the terms by selecting the label which you think best
    justifies each of the documents **2.3** to **2.6**.

4   In what ways would Sir George Buchanan [2.3] and his Government
    have been alarmed by 2.4 and 2.5?

5   In what ways was the Milyukov Note [2.6] offensive to the Soviet
    and why [2.4]?

6   What accusations made against the Bolsheviks can be deduced from
    2.5?

7   How convincing is the Bolshevik evidence that the Provisional
    Government's foreign policy under Milyukov was unchanged from
    that of the Tsar?

8   How does 2.1 differ in character from 2.3–2.6? Evaluate how useful
    the two groups of documents are to historians of the Russian
    revolution.

9   Discuss the view, in the light of the documents above, that it was the
    Soviet which had no meaningful policy towards the war.

The war crisis revealed, both to the majority parties in the Petrograd
Soviet (the Mensheviks and the SRs) and to the majority of the "ten
capitalist ministers" in the Provisional Government, that dual power
could not survive unless the Soviet linked itself more closely to the
Provisional Government. The negotiations for a coalition government
which would include representatives of the Soviet parties led to the
resignations of the Kadet ministers, Milyukov and Guchkov.

2.7   *Izvestia* ('News', paper of the Petrograd Soviet) on the formation of a 'revolutionary government' (16 May 1917)

The Executive Committee of the Soviet of Workers' and Soldiers'
Deputies has come to the conclusion that it is necessary for representatives of the Soviet to join the Provisional Government . . .

   The country is . . . in a dangerous position. Three years of war
have exhausted her strength. Finances are disorganised; railways are   5
broken down; there is a lack of raw materials and fuel, a need of
bread at the front and in the cities – all these have brought on
discontent and mental unrest which tsarist tools are ready to make
use of. The army is breaking up. In certain places a disorderly
seizure of land is going on, a destruction of livestock and implements.   10
Discontent is growing. No one pays any attention to the authorised
agents of the Government. Large masses have no confidence in the
Government, which feels itself powerless and helpless. Only a strong
revolutionary government, enjoying the confidence of the people, can

save the country, hold on to the conquests of the revolution, put an   25
end to the split in the army, and keep it on a war footing.

The Government finds itself in such an unenviable position that
A. I. Guchkov hastens to abandon the sinking ship, and lays down
his title of Minister of War and Navy. But it is not only the
Government but the country itself, that is in a desperate situation . . .   20

This is the reason why the Executive Committee has submitted the
terms on which the representatives of the Soviet would join the
Provisional Government.

From F. A. Golder, *Documents of Russian History* 1914–17, 1964

2.8   The Kronstadt of the countryside. A delegate from Penza reports to the Great Agrarian Committee in Petrograd (July 1917)

Imagine what it is like in our province, with peasants so poor that
they have only a few sazhens [1 sazhen is about $2\frac{1}{2}$ metres] each; how
can a man with a wife and three children live like that? It is no
surprise that, with such small plots, the peasants wanted to improve
their lot as soon as liberty was proclaimed . . . It was for this reason   5
that, following the decisions of our regional soviet on 15 May, the
peasants have changed land ownership even before the meeting of the
Constituent Assembly to legalise its decisions . . . That is how the
land of the proprietors, towns, monasteries, dynasty and the like came to
be managed by local committees, which then shared them out among   10
needy workers. That is what happened to sacrosanct private property.

Obviously not everyone was happy. Those who suffered material or
moral damage were not pleased. A peasant will not bow down any
more and say 'Have pity on me, Ivan Petrovich, my family is dying
of hunger, give me half a desyatin [area of 2.7 acres]' that he will do   15
no more, and instead he will tell you, 'let me know how many
desyatins you can cultivate by yourself, and with your children's help;
come to our meeting tonight and we'll share out the land'. Indeed,
the owners are not happy, not at all (laughter) and they are showering
the local and provincial authorities with complaints, threats of legal   20
action and lamentations. They are trying to poison the atmosphere,
frighten the government and convince it that anarchy has broken
out . . .

And what are the peasants after? They want to safeguard and
better their families, and escape from poverty, above all, but they also   25

understand that the present government of Russia is threatened, and that only the working people can save it, especially the peasantry by taking action and then doing work in exemplary fashion. What is happening among us in Penza is beautiful, artistically beautiful, and I willingly advise all Russia to copy us.   30

Cited in Marc Ferro, *The Bolshevik Revolution – A Social History of the Russian Revolution*, 1985

2.9   Real wages in Petrograd January–October 1917

Month 1917	Price index (1913=1)	Obukhov works			Parviainen			Baltic works		
		nominal wage in rubles	real wage in rubles	as % Jan 1917	nominal wage in rubles	real wage in rubles	as % Jan 1917	nominal wage in rubles	real wage in rubles	as % Jan 1917
January	3.5	160	46	100	144	41	100	86	24	100
April	4.5	192	43	93	212	47.1	115	142	32	133
June	6.0	319	53	115	282	27	114	112	19	79
August	10.5	326	31	67	313	30	73	144	14	58
September	11.4	345	30	65	303	27	66	191	17	70
October	14.3	464	32	69	–	–	–	141	10	42
		Kersten mill			Shaposhnikov tobacco			*Chernorabochie* (Labour exchange data)		
January	3.5	33	10	100	47	13	100	97	28	100
April	4.5	100	22	220	–	–	–	111	24	86
June	6.0	82	14	140	131	22	169	122	20	71
August	10.5	95	9	90	133	13	100	147	14	50
September	11.4	93	8	80	180	16	123	141	12	43
October	14.3	115	9	90	155	11	85	167	12	43

Z. V. Stepanov, *Rabochie Petrograda v period podgotovki i provedeniya oktabr' skogo vooruzhennogo vosstaniya* (Moscow, 1965)

Questions

1   What was the attitude of the Soviet towards the Provisional Government as shown in 2.7? How consistent was the Soviet's policy at this time?

2   Which political party did the delegate from Penza [2.8] most probably support? Explain your choice by reference to his arguments.

3   How far does 2.8 confirm or deny the picture of Russia painted by the Petrograd Soviet [2.7]? What attitude would the Petrograd Soviet have adopted towards the Penza events?

4   Compare the usefulness of **2.8** with an official text like that of the
     Appeal of the Petrograd Soviet **[2.4]** and the table of economic
     statistics **[2.9]**. Explain the relative value of each to a historian.
5   Why is **2.8** particularly important for a study of the events of 1917?

2.10   General Baluev reports on the food supply situation to the Provisional Government

The Commander-in-Chief of the Western Front reports to you that,
following threats by the starving population of the city and uezd
[rural administrative area] to loot and burn down the army storehouses, the commander of the Vyazma Garrison ordered seven
wagons of flour to be removed from the storehouses and made   5
available to the population. Requests, supported by remarks about
possible excesses and *pogroms*, are coming from the food supply
committees in the cities near the front line to provide food for the
population. Hence the front, already in a very serious condition, is
confronted with a great new danger from the starving population. A   10
total break-down in supply is possible. It is now thirteen days since
the ration was fixed at one pound of bread and seven-eighths of a
pound of hardtack [hard biscuit]. During that time there has been a
68 per cent shortfall in deliveries of flour. The hardtack is almost all
gone. We shall have to use the field rations, i.e. deny the front its last 15
supplies for use in case of movement. This may result in serious
consequences. However, the Ministry of Food evidently does not
realise the seriousness of the situation at the front. It does not
provide any tangible help, but merely confirms that the Western
Front is in a sorrowful state.   20

**From M. McCauley, *The Russian Revolution and the Soviet State
1917–21*, 1975**

2.11   A Menshevik worker reports to the local committee of his Party on labour discipline at the Putilov arms factory in Petrograd in September 1917

There is not even a shadow of discipline in the working masses.
Thanks to the replacement of professional guards by soldiers, who are
not quite familiar with the rules for letting workers in and out of the
factory, thefts have become more frequent recently. The number of
instance of workers being drunk is also increasing. But what is most   5

terrible, is the sharp fall in the productivity of labour. Just how low this is, is shown, for example, by the fact that formerly 200 gun carriages were produced each month. But now at most there are 50 to 60. The situation is complicated by purely objective factors, the most important of which is the shortage of fuel and materials ... The   10
Putilov works is in debt to the state to the tune of about 200 million roubles and is hurtling towards the abyss.

Rabochaya Gazeta, **174**, 30 September 1917

Questions

1   Trace the pattern of real wage fluctuations in 1917 [**2.9**]. How do you account for the changes in wage levels?
2   How far do **2.8–2.11** confirm or deny the picture of impending 'ruin' facing the country portrayed by the Soviet leaders in **2.7**? How convincing was the Soviet's proposal for arresting this ruin?
3   Compare **2.9** and **2.10**. Which is the most useful to a historian of 1917 and which reveals the greatest problem facing the working population in 1917?
4   What were the problems facing the Provisional Government in 1917? Explain why the various ministries were unable to solve them?

The July Days and the Kornilov Affair

The accumulation of the grievances of the workers and soldiers of Petrograd finally matured with the so-called 'July Days'. What are the July Days?

2.12(a)   The July Days from the memoirs of a Bolshevik leader of the sailors at Kronstadt

Despite the proved participation of the Anarchists, who senselessly strove to inflame passions, it was not they who initiated the demonstrations: that was beyond the power of such an uninfluential group. The July events took place quite spontaneously, without stimulation from outside. The working class and the peasantry in soldiers' and   5
sailors' greatcoats sensed with their sound instinct that the Provisional Government was destroying the revolution, leading it to the abyss.

   The criminal offensive of June 18 [launched by the Provisional Government, on the Eastern Front], dictated by the vultures of the   10 international stock-exchange and signifying continuation of the war for the old aims of imperialism, together with the treacherous policy of being pursued inside the country, opened the eyes for the masses better than any agitators could. And without waiting for any call, on July 3 they surged on to the streets on their own initiative.   15

How did the Bolshevik Party react to this? On July 2 and 3 it strove with all the influence it possessed to hold back the masses who followed it. In the afternoon of July 3 the Central Committee had printed an appeal to the people to refrain from action. But the electrification of the worker masses and the pressure they exercised   20 was so great, and their collective will was so strikingly manifested in an independent action by some units and the sympathetic action of others which had not yet come out but were ready to do so at any moment, that in the evening of July 4 the Party of the revolutionary proletariat, accurately reflecting the interests and feelings of the   25 worker masses, decided to put itself at the head of the unavoidable movement and, by introducing consciousness into its spontaneity, to transfer it into a peaceful and organised armed demonstration.

F. F. Raskolnikov, *Kronstadt and Petrograd in 1917*, 1962

2.12(b)   A Cartoon from *Petrogradskaia Gazeta* (7 July 1917), labelled 'A High Post for the Leaders of the Rebellion'. The caption below it reads, 'Lenin wants a high post? ... Well? A position is ready for him!!!'

Questions

1   Who, according to Raskolnikov [**2.12(a)**], started the July Days? How valid do you think this conclusion is?
2   What was the main criticism of the Provisional Government at this time [**2.12(a)**]?
3   What role did the Bolshevik Party play in the July Days, according to Raskolnikov?
4   What criteria must we take into consideration when evaluating the accuracy of **2.12(a)**?
5   What were the political opinions of the owners of the Petrogradskaia Gazeta [**2.12(b)**]?
6   How seriously did the cartoon take the threat of Bolshevism? How effectively does it convey this threat?
7   How useful is **2.12(b)** as evidence of the political situation in Russia in 1917?
8   'It was Bolshevik slogans rather than the Bolsheviks which brought about the July Days.' Discuss.

No sooner had Kerensky crushed the threat from the Left than he was faced by a threat from the Right, led by the man he had appointed Commander-in-chief of the Army. When Kornilov led his army on Petrograd, Kerensky dismissed him. Kornilov's response was the following proclamation.

2.13   General Kornilov's Proclamation

People of Russia, our great country is dying. Her end is near. Forced to speak openly, I, General Kornilov, declare that the Provisional Government, under the pressure of the Bolshevik majority in the Soviets, is acting in complete harmony with the German General Staff and, simultaneously with the expected landing of the enemy troops near Riga, is killing the army and shaking the country.   5

The terrible conviction of the inevitable ruin of the country compels me in these frightful times to call upon all Russians to save their dying land. All in whose breast a Russian heart beats, all who believe in God, in the Church, pray to Him for the greatest miracle – the saving of our native land.   10

I, General Kornilov, son of a Cossack peasant, declare to one and all that I desire nothing for myself other than the salvation of our Great Russia, and vow to lead the people, through victory over

enemies, to the Constituent Assembly, where it can determine its   15
future destiny and the form of its future political life.

I cannot betray Russia into the hands of her ancient enemy, the
Germans, who would make slaves of the Russian people. I prefer to
die honourably on the field of battle so that I may not see the shame
and degradation of our Russian land.   20

People of Russia, the life of your native land is in your hands.

General Kornilov

From *Novoe Vremia* (11 September 1917). Translated in F. A. Golder,
Documents of Russian History 1914–17, 1964

2.14   The formation of the Red Guards and the defeat of the Kornilov Revolt

'Notwithstanding the fact that they [the Bolsheviks] are in a minority,' writes Sukhanov [a Menshevik], 'it was clear that in the Military
Revolutionary Committee the leadership belonged to the Bolsheviks.'
He explains this as follows: '. . . only the Bolsheviks had genuine
resources,' for the masses were with them. Intensity in the struggle   5
has everywhere and always brought forth the more active and bolder
elements. This automatic selection inevitably elevated the Bolsheviks,
strengthened their influence, concentrated the initiative in their
hands, giving them de facto leadership even in those organisations
where they were in a minority. The nearer you came to the district,   10
to the factory, to the barrack, the more complete and indubitable was
the leadership of the Bolsheviks. All the nuclei of the party were on
their toes . . . Under direct pressure from the Bolsheviks and the
organisations led by them, the Committee of Defence recognised the
desirability of arming individual groups of workers for the defence of   15
the workers' quarters, the shops and factories. It was only this
sanction that the masses lacked. In the districts, according to the
workers' press, there immediately appeared 'whole queues of people
eager to join the ranks of the Red Guard'. Drilling began in marks-
manship and the handling of weapons. Experienced soldiers were   20
brought in as teachers. By the 29th [August] Guards had been
formed in almost all the districts. The Red Guard announced its
readiness to put in the field a force of 40,000 rifles. The unarmed
workers formed companies for trench-digging, sheetmetal fortifica-
tion, barbed wire fencing.   25

From L. Trotsky, *History of the Russian Revolution*, 1977

Questions

1   What did General Kornilov say was his aim in marching on Petrograd [2.13]?

2   How would 2.13 have been most typically greeted by:
(i) a Petrograd worker?
(ii) a soldier in Petrograd?
(iii) a member of the Kadet Party?
(iv) a supporter of the ex-Tsar?

3   How damaging was 2.13 to Prime Minister Kerensky, and why?

4   If the masses were with the Bolsheviks [2.14, line 5] why did they not have a majority on the Military Revolutionary Committee in August 1917?

5   In what ways did the Kornilov revolt aid the Bolsheviks [2.14]?

6   Which of the two documents 2.13 and 2.14 do you find
(i) more honest
(ii) more useful
on the events of the Kornilov Affair? Give reasons for your choice.

7   'War weariness accounted for the strength of Bolshevism by September 1917.' Discuss.

3 The Bolsheviks and the October Revolution

Lenin and the April Theses

When the revolution broke out in Russia Lenin found himself in exile in Zurich, cut off by the war. He could not return through France or Italy since he had already proclaimed many times that if the Bolsheviks came to power he would take Russia out of the war. The only hope was to go through Germany. The Kaiser's government were only too pleased to assist chaos inside Russia. They not only allowed Lenin to cross Germany (in the legendary 'sealed train') but also groups of Mensheviks, anarchists and SRs who took two later trains. In July, with Bolshevik popularity rising, Lenin was to be labelled a 'German spy' by the Kerensky Government. But in April 1917, when he arrived at the Finland station in the heart of the workers district, the Vyborg, he was given a hero's welcome.

3.1 The Menshevik, Sukhanov, witnesses the arrival of Lenin in Petrograd, 3 April 1917

> . . . Lenin came, or rather ran into the room. He wore a round cap, his face looked frozen, and there was a magnificent bouquet in his hands. Running to the middle of the room, he stopped in front of Chkheidze [a Menshevik leader in the Petrograd Soviet] as though colliding with a completely unexpected obstacle. And Chkheidze, still 5
> glum, pronounced the following 'speech of welcome' with not only the spirit and wording but also the tone of a sermon: 'Comrade Lenin, in the name of the Petersburg Soviet and of the whole revolution we welcome you to Russia . . . But – we think that the principal task of the revolutionary democracy is now the defence of 10
> the revolution from any encroachments either from within or without. We consider that what this goal requires is not disunity, but the closing of the democratic ranks. We hope you will pursue these goals together with us.'

Chkheidze stopped speaking. I was dumbfounded with surprise: 15
really, what attitude could be taken to this 'welcome' and to that
delicious 'But – . . .?' But Lenin clearly knew exactly how to behave
. . . looking about him, examining the persons round him and even
the ceiling of the imperial waiting room, adjusting his bouquet (rather
out of tune with his whole appearance), and then, turning away from   20
the Ex. Com. delegation altogether, he made his reply: 'Dear comrades, soldiers, sailors, and workers! I am happy to greet in your
persons the victorious Russian revolution, and greet you as the vanguard of the world-wide proletarian army . . . The piratical imperialist
war is the beginning of civil war throughout Europe . . . The hour is   25
not far distant when at the call of our comrade, Karl Liebknecht [the
leader of the anti-war German socialists], the peoples will turn their
arms against their own capitalist exploiters . . . The world-wide socialist revolution has already dawned . . . Germany is seething . . . Any
day now the whole of European capitalism may crash. The Russian   30
revolution accomplished by you has prepared the way and opened a
new epoch. Long live the world-wide socialist revolution!' . . .

It was very interesting! Suddenly, before the eyes of all of us,
completely swallowed up by the routine drudgery of the revolution,
there presented a bright, blinding, exotic beacon, obliterating every-   35
thing we 'lived by'. Lenin's voice, heard straight from the train, was
a 'voice from outside'.

**N. N. Sukhanov, *The Russian Revolution 1917. A Personal Memoir*,
edited and translated by Joel Carmichael, 1955**

Sukhanov was not the only observer in Petrograd to be surprised by
Lenin's speech. *Pravda*, the Bolshevik paper, had been echoing the
sentiments of the Mensheviks in supporting the Provisional Government
and the war effort, ever since Stalin, Kamenev and Muranov had arrived
back from Siberia in March. Now Lenin aimed to change the programme
which the Bolsheviks had pursued since 1903. In *The Tasks of the
Proletariat in Our Revolution*, popularly known as the April Theses, Lenin
set out the new priorities. On page 66 is an extract from them which
deals with the most important issues.

3.2 The April Theses

1 In our attitude towards the war, which under the new government of Lvov and Co. unquestionably remains on Russia's part a predatory imperialist war owing to the capitalist nature of that government, not the slightest concession to 'revolutionary defencism' is possible . . .

2 The specific feature of the present situation in Russia is that the country is PASSING from the first stage of the revolution – which, owing to the insufficient class-consciousness and organisation of the proletariat, placed power in the hands of the bourgeoisie – to its SECOND stage, which must place power in the hands of the proletariat and the poorest sections of the peasants . . .

3 No support for the Provisional Government; the utter falsity of all its promises should be made clear, particularly of those relating to the renunciation of annexations. Exposure in place of the impermissible, illusion-breeding 'demand' that THIS government, a government of capitalists, should cease to be an imperialist government . . .

4 The masses be made to see that the Soviets of Workers Deputies are the ONLY POSSIBLE form of revolutionary government, and that therefore our task is, as long as THIS government yields to the influence of the bourgeoisie, to present a patient, systematic, and persistent EXPLANATION of the errors of their tactics . . .

5 Not a parliamentary republic – to return to a parliamentary republic from the Soviet of Workers' Deputies would be a retrograde step – but a republic of Workers', Agricultural Labourers' and Peasants' Deputies throughout the country, from top to bottom.
Abolition of the police, the army and the bureaucracy.
The salaries of all officials, all of whom are elective and displaceable at any time not to exceed the average wage of a competent worker.

6 The weight of emphasis in the agrarian programme to be shifted to the Soviet of Agricultural Labourers' Deputies.
Confiscation of all landed estates.
Nationalisation of ALL lands in the country, the land to be disposed of by the local Soviets of Agricultural Labourers' and Peasants' Deputies . . .

7   The immediate amalgamation of all banks in the country into a   40
    single national bank . . .
8   It is not our IMMEDIATE task to 'introduce' socialism, but
    only to bring social production and the distribution of products
    at once under the CONTROL of the Soviets of Workers'
    Deputies.   45
9   Party tasks:
    (a) Immediate convocation of a party congress
    (b) Alteration of the party programme . . .
    (c) Change of the party's name
10 A new International   50

V. I. Lenin, *Collected Works*, vol. 24, 1962

Questions

1   Contrast the speeches of Lenin and Chkheidze in **3.1**. What were the
    main political and emotional differences between them?
2   On whom, and what, in particular, did Lenin base his view of the
    future of the Russian Revolution?
3   Account for the tone of Sukhanov in **3.1**. How reliable a witness was
    he?
4   'The April Theses can be described as a completely socialist pro-
    gramme.' How valid do you think this statement is, and why?
5   Examine **3.1** and **3.2**. Which of them is more useful to historians of
    the Russian Revolution? You should consider the issues of reliability,
    relevance, and purpose.

Lenin's April Theses were defended before a joint meeting of the
Bolsheviks, Mensheviks and independent socialists on the next day
(4 April); in the Bolshevik Central Committee two days later; and in the
first Petrograd City Conference held between 14–22 April. The universal
reaction was shock accompanied by 'mockery, hubbub and laughter'
(Sukhanov). Only Alexandra Kollontai (see Key Personalities) supported
Lenin at the first meeting, whilst the higher echelons of the Bolshevik
Party rejected the April Theses by 13 votes to 2 on 8 April. It was only in
the Petrograd City Conference that Lenin first achieved a majority for his
positions.

3.3(a)   The Menshevik, Bogdanov, responds on 4 April

'This is the raving of a madman! It's indecent to applaud this claptrap!' he cried out, livid with rage and contempt, turning to the audience. 'You ought to be ashamed of yourselves! Marxists!'

N. N. Sukhanov, *The Russian Revolution 1917. A Personal Memoir*, translated and edited by Joel Carmichael, 1955

3.3(b)   The Bolshevik Kamenev rejects the April Theses

As for Comrade Lenin's general scheme, it appears to us unacceptable, inasmuch as it proceeds from the assumption that the bourgeois-democratic revolution is COMPLETED, and builds on the immediate transformation of the revolution into a socialist revolution.

From V. I. Lenin, *Collected Works*, vol. 24, 1962

The enemies of Bolshevism breathed a sigh of relief. Victor Chernov, leader of the Socialist Revolutionary Party and future Minister of Agriculture in the Provisional Government of Kerensky, was convinced that Lenin was out of touch with Russian affairs.

3.3(c)   Chernov comments on Lenin's influence

Let us ... not be unduly frightened by Lenin's political excesses, just because their derivation and character are too clear. The extent of their influence, and consequently also their dangers, will be extremely limited and 'localised'.

From R. Browder and A. Kerensky, *The Russian Provisional Government*, vol. III, 1961

3.3(d)   Ludmila Stal [a member of the Bolshevik Petrograd Central Committee] gives the only vocal support to the April Theses in the Petrograd City Conference

All the comrades before the arrival of Lenin were wandering in the dark. We knew only the formulas of 1905. Seeing the independent creative work of the people, we could not teach them. I turn now to the comrades of the Vyborg district and propose that they learn the full importance of the moment. Our comrades were only able to see   5 as far as preparing for the Constituent Assembly by parliamentary means, and took no account of the possibility of going further. In accepting the slogans of Lenin we are now doing what life suggests to us.

From T. Cliff, *Lenin*, vol. 2, 1975

Questions

1   Why does Bogdanov, a Marxist, snort 'Marxists!' [3.3(a), line 3]?
2   What evidence is there in 3.3(a) and at the Petrograd City Conference [3.3(d)] to indicate that Lenin enjoyed more support than an analysis of the speeches of the time would appear to suggest? What implications are there here for historians of political events?
3   All the documents in 3.3 are from people who, to one degree or another, had been influenced by marxist ideas. In the context of 1917 how would you evaluate their 'marxist orthodoxy'?
4   Evaluate the sources in 3.3. Which would be most reliable as an expression of the views of the individual in question, and why?
5   How do 3.1–3.3 express the dilemma of Russian socialists in 1917? What were the fundamental causes of their problems?

The Bolsheviks plan insurrection

Despite the opposition of most of the Party's Central Committee, Lenin obtained a majority for his position in the Seventh All-Russian Conference of the Bolshevik Party held between 24 and 29 April. The basis of the Bolshevik propaganda was now drawn up around the April Theses and was generally summarised (though not exclusively) in the slogans 'All Power to the Soviets' and 'Bread, Peace and Land'. The importance of these slogans was that they showed that the Bolsheviks had a clear policy on the major issues facing the Russian people in 1917. This contrasted markedly with the Provisional Government's failure to take Russia out of the war and with the failure of the other socialist parties which dominated the Petrograd Soviet at that time to distinguish themselves from the Provisional Government's failures.

As 1917 wore on the Bolsheviks rose in popularity as the other parties' support evaporated. From being a small sect of about 8,000 in 1916, the Bolshevik Party was transformed into a mass party of 170,000 members by the summer of 1917. This, however, does not do justice to the influence which Bolshevik positions had within the working class in general and the soldiers of the Petrograd Garrison in particular. In the factory committees, for example, Bolshevik support was overwhelming.

Of the 25 members of the Petrograd Central Council of Factory Committees, which was formed in June, 1917, 19 were Bolsheviks.

Yet in the same month, Lenin's solemn assurance that the Bolsheviks were ready to assume governmental power provoked only laughter in the Petrograd Soviet. The demonstrations on 18 June against the war made it clear, however, that the Bolsheviks were the only party which had widespread support amongst the workers and soldiers in the capital. Even the July Days was only a temporary setback which did not harm recruitment to the party. It was Lenin who, still hiding in Finland after the July Days, was the first to grasp the opportunity that the Kornilov Affair presented.

3.4 Lenin on the Kornilov Affair

The Kornilov revolt is a ... downright unbelievably sharp turn in events.

Like every sharp turn, it calls for a revision and a change of tactics. And, as with every revision, we must be extra cautious not to become unprincipled ...   5

Even now we must not support Kerensky's government. This is unprincipled. We will be asked: aren't we going to fight against Kornilov? Of course we must! But this is not the same thing; there is a dividing line here, which is being stepped over by some Bolsheviks who fall into compromise and allow themselves to be carried away by 10 the course of events.

We shall fight, we are fighting against Kornilov, just as Kerensky's troops do, but we do not support Kerensky. On the contrary, we expose his weakness. There is the difference. It is a rather subtle difference, but it is highly essential and must not be forgotten ...   15

... we must campaign not so much directly against Kerensky as indirectly against him, namely by demanding a more and more active, truly revolutionary war against Kornilov ... by drawing the masses in, by arousing them, by inflaming them, (Kerensky is afraid of the masses, afraid of the people) ...   20

V. I. Lenin, *Selected Works*, vol. 2, 1977

3.5 Lenin's arguments for planning an insurrection in Petrograd on 10 October

... the decisive moment is near. The international situation is such that we must take the initiative. What is being done to surrender as far as the Narva [District] and to surrender Peter [Petrograd] makes it even more imperative for us to take decisive action. The political position is also working impressively in this direction. On 3–5 July, 5 positive action on our part would have failed because the majority was not behind us. Since then we have gone up in leaps and bounds.

Absenteeism and indifference among the masses can be explained by the fact that the masses are fed up with words and resolutions. The majority is now behind us. Politically, the situation is completely 10 ripe for a transfer of power.

The agrarian movement is going in the same direction, for it is clear that it would need heroic forces to quell this movement. The slogan for all land to be transferred has become the general slogan of all the peasants. So the political circumstances are ripe. We have to 15 talk about the technical side. That is the crux of the matter. Yet we, in the wake of the defencists, are inclined to regard the systematic preparation of an insurrection as something akin to a political sin.

It is senseless to wait for the Constituent Assembly, which will clearly not be on our side, for this means complicating our task. The 20 Regional Congress and the proposal from Minsk must be used as the starting point for decisive action.

From A. Bone (ed.), *The Bolsheviks and the October Revolution.*
Minutes of the Central Committee of the Russian Social Democratic
Labour Party (Bolsheviks) August 1917– February 1918, **1974**

Questions

1   What, according to Lenin [3.5] was the difference between the situation in July and in October?
2   Lenin was described by his Menshevik opponents as a 'putschist'. What is your verdict on this on the basis of the evidence in **3.4** and **3.5**?
3   What was the 'weakness' of Kerensky's position [**3.4, line 14**]?
4   How would Lenin have squared the apparent contradiction that the majority was with the Bolsheviks but the Constituent Assembly was against them?
5   How important are the writings of Lenin as a source of evidence for the Russian Revolution?
6   'Circumstances make the man, not the man the circumstances' (E. H. Carr, *Socialism in One Country*, vol. 1, 1952). Comment on this judgement in the light of the roles of Kerensky and/or Lenin in the Russian Revolution.

3.6   Kamenev and Zinoviev, two of Lenin's oldest associates, print their objections to a Bolshevik insurrection in Gorky's newpaper, *Novaya Zhizn* ('New Life') on 18 October 1917

Not only comrade Zinoviev and I but also a number of comrades
with experience in the field consider it would be inadmissable, and
fatal for the proletariat and the revolution, for us to initiate an armed
insurrection at the present moment, with the prevailing relationship
of social forces, independently of, and only a few days before a   5
Congress of Soviets ... insurrection, in Marx's expression, is an art.
And that is just why we believe that it is our duty now, in the
present circumstances, to speak out against any attempt to initiate an
armed insurrection which would be doomed to defeat and would
bring in its train the most disastrous consequences for the party, for   10
the proletariat, for the destiny of the revolution ... And our party is
too strong, it has too great a future, to take such steps.

From A. Bone (ed.), *The Bolsheviks and the October Revolution*, 1974

The Bolsheviks seize power

3.7   Sukhanov, a Menshevik, describes the Bolshevik takeover of Petrograd on the night of 6/7 November

No resistance was shown. Beginning at 2 in the morning the stations,
bridges, lighting installations, telegraphs and telegraphic agency were
gradually occupied by small forces brought from the barracks. The
little groups of cadets could not resist and didn't think of it. In
general the military operations in the politically important centres of   5
the city rather resembled a changing of the guard. The weaker
defence force, of cadets, retired and a strengthened defence force, of
guards, took its place ... the decisive operations that had begun were
quite bloodless; not one casualty was recorded. The city was absolutely calm. Both the centre and the suburbs were sunk in a deep sleep,   10
not suspecting what was going on in the quiet of the cold autumn
night ... The operations, gradually developing, went so smoothly
that no great forces were required. Out of the garrison of 200,000,
scarcely a tenth went into action, probably much fewer.

**N. N. Sukhanov, *The Russian Revolution 1917. A Personal Memoir*,
translated and edited by Joel Carmichael, 1955**

3.8   Description of the October Revolution by the leader of the Kadet Party, Milyukov

At dawn on November 7 Kerensky was able to ascertain that the revolution had broken out and that Supreme Headquarters had done nothing to defend Petrograd. He blamed the military for having been complacent. He then transferred to Kishkin, the minister of civil affairs, the command of the women's battalion, called the 'Shock   5
Battalion', and the detachments formed by the students of the military academy, who were assembled before the Winter Palace. Kerensky then hastened from the capital under the protection of an automobile of the American Embassy, to go out to meet the troops that had been recalled from the front. Toward the end of the after-   10
noon the Winter Palace was surrounded and no longer could communicate with the city. The Provisional Government in vain awaited Kerensky's return with the troops. At night the cruiser Aurora, which had gone over to the Bolsheviks after its arrival from Kronstadt, bombarded the Palace ...   15

Finally, the sailors, soldiers and workers of the Red Guard penetrated the Palace, and the commander surrendered on the condition that they spare the lives of the cadets. The members of the Provisional Government were ... imprisoned in the fortress of St. Peter and St. Paul where they again met the ministers of the Tsarist   20
regime, who had been imprisoned by the March Revolution.

It was similarly the irony of fate that Kerensky asked for help from the same troops that had marched on Petrograd in September to execute Kornilov's plan. What had happened under Kornilov was repeated exactly but still more rapidly. The troops, composed largely   25
of Cossacks, did not wish to fight for Kerensky, and dispersed ...

General dissolution [of Russia] began under the Provisional Government ... The disorganisation resulting from the extraordinary military effort, the extreme lassitude of the army, the economic disarray, all this prepared Russia for Bolshevism ... Lenin had only   30
to sanction an accomplished fact to assure the sympathy of the soldiers, peasants and workers.

From P. A. Milyukov, *History of the Second Russian Revolution*, 1959

Questions

1   Milyukov was a former cabinet colleague of Kerensky in the Pro-
     visional Government (see chapter 2). What attitudes does he reveal
     towards his former colleague in **3.8**? How do you account for his
     attitudes?

2   Does Milyukov successfully account for the victory of the Bolsheviks?
     Explain your answer.

3   Milyukov was a Professor of History as well as the leader of the
     Kadet Party from 1905 until 1918. Does this mean we should dis-
     count his testimony either as an eyewitness or as an historian?
     Explain your conclusions.

4   According to Trotsky the October Revolution 'was the most popular
     mass insurrection in all history. The workers had no need to come
     out into the public square in order to fuse together: they were already
     one single whole without that' (*The History of the Russian Revolution*.
     How far do **3.7** and **3.8** confirm or deny this view?

5   'It was the failure of their opponents rather than the strengths of the
     Bolsheviks which led to their victory in October.' Discuss with refer-
     ence to the actions of the Mensheviks, the Provisional Government,
     the army, Kerensky and the Bolsheviks themselves.

Lenin had called for the overthrow of the Provisional Government before
the Second All-Russian Congress of Soviets would meet on 7 November.
This is largely what happened, except that the beleaguered Ministers in
the Winter Palace held out until after the Congress began. Because of the
symbolic value of this final surrender, the Second Congress thus opened
with some confusion.

However, there was no doubt that Bolshevik delegates had won an
overwhelming majority in the Congress. A new Executive Committee (or
ExCom) was quickly elected on a proportional basis. This meant that the
Bolsheviks with 14 seats, compared with all the other parties combined
total of 10, would dominate. This domination increased when the Left SRs
announced that, unlike the Right SRs, who had walked out, they would
support the idea of Soviet power. Lenin, still in disguise, was waiting in
the adjoining room. One by one the delegates of the minor parties, the
former dominant parties in the Soviet, got up to denounce the Bolshevik
insurrection. As Martov, collaborator of Lenin until 1903, rose to speak,
the rumble of the cruiser Aurora's guns as it fired on the Winter Palace
could be heard. This roused Martov to a fierce attack on the Bolsheviks
for creating civil war (like everyone else in the Soviet he did not know

that the cruiser was firing blanks). More seriously for the Bolsheviks, Martov also proposed a new search for compromise which called for the Right SRs and Mensheviks to have a say in the new government.

3.9   The Menshevik Internationalists [the left-wing of the Mensheviks] and their allies leave the Second Congress of Soviets

> But it was necessary to put up a resistance to Martov. This task fell to Trotsky. The opponents stand side by side in the tribune, hemmed in on all sides by excited delegates. 'What has taken place,' says Trotsky, 'is an insurrection, not a conspiracy. An insurrection of the popular masses needs no justification. We have tempered and   5
> hardened the revolutionary energy of the Petrograd workers and soldiers. We have openly forged the will of the masses to insurrection and not conspiracy ... Our insurrection has conquered, and now you propose to us: renounce your victory; make a compromise. With whom? I ask: With whom ought we to make a compromise? With   10
> that pitiful handful that just went out? Haven't we seen them through and through. There is no longer anybody in Russia who is for them. Are the millions of workers and peasants represented in this Congress ... to enter a compromise with these men? No, a compromise is no good here. To those who have gone out, and to all who make like   15
> proposals, we must say, "You are pitiful isolated individuals; you are bankrupts; your role is played out. Go where you belong from now on – into the rubbish can of history!" '
> 'Then we will go!' cries Martov, without awaiting the vote of the Congress.   20

L. Trotsky, *The History of the Russian Revolution*, 1977

Some Menshevik Internationalists did not leave (though Sukhanov and the stenographers who recorded the proceedings did). Thus the only record that we have of the second day of the Congress was written by the American journalist and future Communist, John Reed. Whilst the Bolshevik leaders spent the day deliberating about the nature of the new government, the Military Revolutionary Committee, which had actually co-ordinated the insurrection, started to issue proclamations, closing down the right-wing newspapers (but not the socialist ones) and generally preparing Petrograd for the expected counter-attack by Kerensky. The Winter Palace had fallen in the early hours of the morning but the next session of the Second Soviet Congress did not reconvene until the evening of 8 November.

3.10   Lenin's reappearance in public for the first time for 5 months

It was just 8.40 when a thundering wave of cheers announced the
entrance of the presidium, with Lenin – great Lenin – among them. A
short, stocky figure with a big head set down on his shoulders, bald
and bulging. Little eyes, a snubbish nose, wide generous mouth, and
heavy chin; clean-shaven now but already beginning to bristle with   5
the well-known beard of his past and future. Dressed in shabby
clothes, his trousers much too long for him. Unimpressive, to be the
idol of a mob, loved and revered as perhaps few leaders in history
have been. A strange popular leader – a leader purely by virtue of
intellect; colourless, humourless, uncompromising and detached,   10
without picturesque idiosyncrasies – but with the power of explaining
profound ideas in simple terms, of analysing a concrete situation.
And, combined with shrewdness, the greatest intellectual audacity ...
... gripping the edge of the reading stand, letting his little winking
eyes travel over the crowd as he stood there waiting, apparently   15
oblivious to the long-rolling ovation, which lasted several minutes.
When it finished he said simply, 'We shall now proceed to construct
the Socialist order!' Again that overwhelming human roar.

John Reed, *Ten Days that Shook the World*, 1926

The Bolsheviks hastened to keep their promises. On that very night of
8 November the Decree on Peace, personally drafted by Lenin, was
brought before the Congress. The actual decree is printed later [5.1].

Questions

1   What distinction did Trotsky make in **3.9** between a conspiracy and
    an insurrection? How valid do you think this distinction was?
2   What 'compromise' was Martov trying to propose [**3.9, line 9**]? Why
    did Trotsky reject it?
3   Of all Lenin's characteristics mentioned in **3.10**, which did the author
    believe to be the secret of his personal influence?
4   'After their deaths, attempts are made to convert them into harmless
    icons, to canonise them, so to speak, to render a certain homage to
    their names ...' (Lenin). Does this mean that the role of individuals
    like Lenin should be discounted from historical enquiry as unimpor-
    tant? Did Lenin shape the course of the Russian Revolution or was
    he an opportunist responding to circumstances?
5   'Coup d'état or popular rising?' Which description best characterises
    the October Revolution, and why?

4 The nature of the Soviet State

The Bolsheviks were well aware that seizing power was much easier than holding it. They knew too that they faced enormous problems but believed that in achieving peace and sanctioning the seizure of the land by local peasant Soviets they had the solutions for Russia. Above all, they believed that these policies were only necessary until the international working class revolution came to the rescue of the workers' state. In the next three chapters we will look at the political, military and economic problems which confronted the Bolshevik Government during the period of the civil war, which ended in December 1920.

A new form of government?

The Bolsheviks were the only politically organised group which supported the concept of 'Soviet power', but the exact nature of this form of government had not been discussed in advance of the overthrow of the Provisional Government. Document **4.1** is dated from 3 November, only four days before the October Revolution itself. The second was written by Lenin in hiding in Finland in August and September 1917.

4.1 Bolshevik anticipation of a majority in the Second Congress of Soviets for power to pass to the Soviets. John Reed at the Smolny Institute.

> In the corridor I met Karakhan, member of the Bolshevik Central Committee, who explained to me what the new government would be like.
> 'A loose organisation, sensitive to the popular will as expressed through the Soviets, allowing local forces full play. At present the   5
> Provisional Government obstructs the action of the local democratic will, just as the Tsar's Government did. The initiative of the new society shall come from below ... The form of the Government will be modelled on the constitution of the Russian Social Democratic Labour Party. The new Tsay-ee-kah [Executive committee] respon-   10
> sible to frequent meetings of the All-Russian Congress of Soviets,

will be the parliament; the various ministries will be headed by collegia – committees – instead of by Ministers, and will be directly responsible to the Soviets ...'

John Reed, *Ten Days that Shook the World*, 1926

4.2 From *The State and Revolution*

The way out of parliamentarism is not, of course, the abolition of representative institutions and the elective principle, but the conversion of representative institutions from talking shops into 'working' bodies. 'The Commune was to be a working, not a parliamentary, body, executive and legislative at the same time.'*   5

'A working, not a parliamentary body' – this is a blow straight from the shoulder at the present-day parliamentarians and parliamentary 'lap dogs' of Social Democracy! Take any parliamentary country from America to Switzerland, from France to Britain, Norway and so forth – in these countries the real business of the 'state' is performed   10 behind the scenes and is carried on by the departments, chancelleries and General Staffs. Parliament is given up to talk for the special purpose of fooling the 'common people'.

This is so true that even in the Russian Republic, a bourgeois-democratic republic, all these sins of parliamentarism came out at   15 once even before it managed to set up a real parliament ... In the Soviet, the 'socialist' Ministers are fooling the credulous rustics with phrase-mongering and resolutions. In the government itself a sort of permanent shuffle is going on in order that, on the one hand, as many Socialist-Revolutionaries and Mensheviks as possible may in turn get   20 near the 'pie', the lucrative and honourable posts and that, on the other hand, the 'attention' of the people may be 'engaged'. Meanwhile the chancelleries and army staffs 'do' the business of 'state'.

V. I. Lenin, *Selected Works*, vol. 2, 1977

---

* The quotation is from Karl Marx's *The Civil War in France* (1872) which Lenin was analysing to draw lessons for the shape of the future 'dictatorship of the proletariat'.

4.3 The Decree of the Second All-Russian Congress of Soviets to form the Workers' and Peasants' Government, 8 November 1917

The All-Russian Congress of Soviets of Workers', Soldiers' and
Peasants' Deputies resolves:

To establish a Provisional Workers' and Peasants' Government, to
be known as the Council of Peoples Commissars [or *Sovnarkom* from
its abbreviated name in Russian], to govern the country until the   5
Constituent Assembly is convened. The management of individual
branches of state activity is entrusted to commissions whose members
shall ensure the fulfilment of the programme announced by the
Congress, and shall work in close contact with mass organisations of
men and women workers, sailors, soldiers, peasants and office   10
employees. Governmental authority is vested in a collegium of the
chairmen of those commissions, i.e. the Council of People's
Commissars.

Control over the activities of the People's Commissars with the
right to replace them is vested in the All-Russia Congress of Soviets   15
of Workers', Peasants' and Soldiers' Deputies and its Central Executive Committee.

At the present time the Council of People's Commissars is consti-
tuted as follows:

Chairman of the Council – Vladimir Ulyanov (Lenin);   20
People's Commissar of the Interior – A. I. Rykov;
Agriculture – V. P. Milyutin;
Labour – A. G. Shlyapnikov;
Army and Navy Affairs – a committee consisting of V. A.
    Ovseenko (Antonov), N. V. Krylenko and P. Y. Dybenko;   25
Commerce and Industry – V. P. Nogin;
Finance – I. Skvortsov (Stepanov);
Foreign Affairs – L. D. Bronstein (Trotsky);
Justice – G. I. Oppokov (Lomov);
Food – I. A. Teodorovich;   30
Post and Telegraphs – N. P. Avilov (Glebov);
Chairman for Nationalities Affairs – J. V. Djugashvili (Stalin).

The office of People's Commissar of Railways is temporarily vacant.

Y. Akhapkin, *First Decrees of Soviet Power*, 1970

Questions

1   What did Marx mean by saying that the Commune would combine 'executive' and 'legislative' powers [**4.2, line 5**]? How are these powers distinguished in modern western parliamentary democratic states?

2   Outline the differences and similarities between the visions for the future of Karakhan [**4.1**] and Lenin [**4.2**]?

3   How accurate was Lenin's accusation in **4.2, line 21** that the other socialists were simply after a share of the 'pie'? Explain your judgement.

4   Why, after six months of a democratic revolution, had Russia no 'real parliament' [**4.2, line 16**]? How far was this a factor in the success of the Bolsheviks?

5   How far did the decree on the form of the workers' and peasants' government [**4.3**] conform to the ideals set out in **4.1** and **4.2**, and in what ways?

6   'For the Bolsheviks "Soviet democracy" was a mere convenience to hide their thirst for power.' Discuss.

Lenin's views on the revolution

It is interesting to look at the evolution of Lenin's views on the nature of the revolution and the role of the ordinary worker in it.

4.4(a)   Lenin on the dictatorship of the proletariat and the withering away of the State (September 1917)

... the transition from capitalist society – which is developing towards communism – to communist society is impossible without a 'political transition period', and the state in this period can only be the revolutionary dictatorship of the proletariat.

What then is the relationship of this dictatorship to democracy? ... 5
Democracy for an insignificant minority, democracy for the rich – that is the democracy of capitalist society. If we look more closely into the machinery of capitalist democracy, we see everywhere, in the 'petty' – supposedly petty – details of the suffrage (residential qualification, exclusion of women, etc.), in the technique of the representa-   10
tive institutions, in actual obstacles to the right of assembly (public buildings are not for 'paupers'!), in the purely capitalist organisation of the daily press, etc., etc. – we see restriction after restriction upon democracy ...

And so in capitalist society we have a democracy that is curtailed,   15
wretched, false, a democracy only for the rich, for the minority. The
dictatorship of the proletariat, the period of transition to communism,
will for the first time create democracy for the people, for the
majority, along with the necessary suppression of the exploiters, of
the minority. Communism alone is capable of providing really com-   20
plete democracy, and the more complete it is, the sooner it will
become unnecessary and wither away of its own accord.

V. I. Lenin, 'The State and Revolution', *Selected Works*, vol. 2, 1977

4.4(b) Lenin in November 1917

Creative activity at the grass roots is the basic factor of the new
public life. Let the workers set up workers' control at their factories.
Let them supply the villages with manufactures in exchange for grain
. . . Socialism cannot be decreed from above. Its spirit rejects the
mechanical bureaucratic approach; living creative socialism is the   5
product of the masses themselves.

Quoted in N. Harding, *Lenin's Political Thought*, vol. 1, 1983

4.4(c) Lenin at the Third Congress of Soviets in January 1918

It is important for us to draw literally all working people into the
government of the state. It is a task of tremendous difficulty. But
socialism cannot be implemented by a minority, by the Party. It can
be implemented only by tens of millions when they have learned to
do it for themselves.   5

Quoted in N. Harding, *Lenin's Political Thought*, vol. 1, 1983

4.4(d) *The Immediate Tasks of the Soviet Government* written in April 1918

Without the guidance of experts in the various fields of knowledge,
technology and experience, the transition to socialism will be impossible, because socialism calls for a conscious mass advance to greater
productivity of labour compared with capitalism . . . And the specialists, because of the whole social environment that made them specia-   5
lists, are, in the main, inevitably bourgeois . . .

Now we have to resort to the old bourgeois methods and to agree
to pay a very high price for the 'services' of the top bourgeois
experts . . .

Clearly this measure is a compromise, a departure from the princi-   10
ples of the Paris Commune [1871] and of every proletarian power . . .

V. I. Lenin, *Selected Works*, vol. 2, 1977

**4.4(e)   Lenin in the summer of 1918 when famine began to sweep
through urban areas**

THE PRIMARY TASK IN A RUINED COUNTRY IS TO SAVE
THE WORKING PEOPLE. THE PRIMARY PRODUCTIVE
FORCE OF HUMAN SOCIETY AS A WHOLE, IS THE
WORKERS, THE WORKING PEOPLE. If they survive, we shall
save and restore EVERYTHING . . . We must save the workers even   5
if they are unable to work. If we keep them alive for the next few
years we shall save the country, save society and socialism.

Quoted in N. Harding, *Lenin's Political Thought*, vol. 2, 1983

4.4(f)   Lenin in December 1920

. . . the dictatorship of the proletariat cannot be exercised through an
organisation embracing the whole of that class, because in all capitalist countries (and not only over here, in one of the most backward)
the proletariat is still so divided, so degraded and so corrupted . . .
that an organisation taking in the whole of the proletariat cannot   5
directly exercise proletarian dictatorship. It can be exercised only by
a vanguard that has absorbed the revolutionary energy of the class.

Quoted in N. Harding, *Lenin's Political Thought*, vol. 2, 1983

**4.4(g)   Lenin in his last article 'Better Fewer but Better'
(March 1923)**

We must reduce our state apparatus to the utmost degree of economy. We must banish from it all traces of extravagance, of which so
much has been left over from Tsarist Russia, from its bureaucratic
capitalist state machine.

V. I. Lenin, *Selected Works*, vol. 3, 1977

Questions

1   What is the basis of Lenin's critique of democracy under capitalist regimes?
2   From the extracts given in **4.2** and **4.4** summarise Lenin's views on democracy, dictatorship and the Paris Commune.
3   Trace the development of Lenin's views on the evolution of the Soviet state as represented in **4.4**. Explain how and why this development took place.
4   Using this and the following chapters, draw up a timeline for the main events in the political, military, economic and international spheres between November 1917 and March 1921. How far do Lenin's political utterances reflect events in areas other than the political?

The Constituent Assembly meets, January 1918

On 26 December Lenin published in *Pravda* his 'Theses on the Constituent Assembly' which began by maintaining that 'a republic of Soviets is a higher form of democracy than the usual bourgeois republic with a Constituent Assembly'. He went on to call for fresh elections, but only after the Assembly proclaimed 'that it unreservedly recognises Soviet power, the Soviet Revolution, and its policy on the questions of peace, the land and workers' control . . .' (*Selected Works*, vol. 2). The scene was thus set for a confrontation when the Constituent Assembly opened on 18 January 1918.

4.5(a)   The results of the elections to the Constituent Assembly

	Votes		Delegates
Socialist-Revolutionaries	16,500,000	Right	299
		Left	39
Bolsheviks	9,023,963		168
Ukrainian and other SRs	4,400,000		81
Conservative and nationalists	2,750,000		83
Kadets	1,856,639		15
Lesser Social Democrats (including Mensheviks)	1,700,000		18

Based on Figures in M. Liebman, *Leninism under Lenin*, 1975, and W. H. Chamberlin, *The Russian Revolution 1917–21*, 1935, vol. 1

4.5(b)   Election returns in Petrograd to the Constituent Assembly

RESULTS IN PETROGRAD		Delegates elected
Bolshevik vote	415,587	6
Kadet vote	245,628	4
SRs vote	149,644	2
All other parties' vote	117,495	0
Total vote	928,354	12

DRIFT OF PUBLIC OPINION IN PETROGRAD ELECTIONS

Leading Parties	September 2 Total	%	November 25 Total	%
SRs	205,665	38	149,644	16
Bolsheviks	183,694	33	415,587	45
Kadets	114,485	21	245,628	26
Others	45,534	8	117,495	13
Total vote	549,378	100	928,354	100

VOTE OF NOVEMBER 25

Leading Parties	Civilian Wards Total	%	Military Wards Total	%
SRs	139,644	16	9,980	12
Bolsheviks	347,719	43	67,868	76
Kadets	240,693	28	4,935	6
Others	112,081	13	5,414	6
Total vote	840,157	100	88,197	100

Leading Parties	July 8 Total	%	October 3 Total	%	December 2–4 Total	%
SRs	375,000	58	54,000	14	62,000	8
Bolsheviks	75,000	12	198,000	51	366,000	48
Kadets	109,000	17	101,000	26	264,000	35
Others	108,000	13	[?]		43,000	9
Total vote	667,000		[?]		735,000	

Table title: DRIFT OF PUBLIC OPINION IN MOSCOW ELECTIONS

Based on J. Bunyan and H. H. Fisher, *The Bolshevik Revolution 1917–1918*, 1934

When the Constituent Assembly did meet, the Kadets had already been outlawed for supporting the civil war that had been started by the Cossack General Kaledin. The Bolsheviks had proposed Maria Spiridonova of the Left SRs as the Chair, but the Right SRs had ensured a majority for their delegation and duly elected the SR leader, Chernov. Chernov had been a Minister of Agriculture under the Provisional Government during which time he had not carried out his Party's programme of giving land to the peasants that worked it. This is his account of the meeting.

4.6   Chernov on 'Russia's One Day Parliament'

When we, the newly elected members of the Constituent Assembly, entered the Tauride Palace, the seat of the Assembly at Petrograd on 18 January 1918, we found that the corridors were full of armed guards. At first they did not address us directly, and only exchanged casual observations to the effect that 'This guy should get a bayonet   5 between his ribs' or 'It wouldn't be bad to put some lead into this one' . . .

I delivered my inauguration address making vigorous efforts to keep self-control. Every sentence of my speech was met with outcries, some ironical, others spiteful, often buttressed by the brandishing of   10 guns . . .

I finished my speech amidst a cross-fire of interruptions and cries. It was now the turn of the Bolshevik speakers . . . During their

delivery our sector was a model of restraint and self-discipline. We
maintained a cold dignified silence. The Bolshevik speeches as usual   15
were shrill, clamorous, provocative and rude, but they could not
break the icy silence . . .

Lenin, in the government box, demonstrated his contempt for the
Assembly by lounging in his chair and putting on the air of a man
who was bored to death . . .   20

When it appeared that we refused to vote the Soviet 'Platform'
without discussion the Bolsheviks walked out of the sitting in a body
. . . I felt sure we would be arrested. But it was of utmost importance
for us to have a chance to say the last word. I declared that the next
point on the agenda was the land reform. At this moment somebody   25
pulled at my sleeve.

I proceeded to read the main paragraphs of the Land Bill, which
our party had prepared long ago. But time was running short.
Reports and debates had to be omitted. Upon my proposal the
Assembly voted six basic points of the bill. It provided that all land   30
was to be turned into common property, with every tiller possessing
equal rights to use it. Amidst incessant shouts: 'That's enough!', 'Stop
it now!', 'Clear the hall!' the other points of the bill were voted . . .

In the dawn of a foggy and murky morning I declared recess until
noon . . .   35

At noon several members of the Assembly were sent on reconnais-
sance. They reported that the door of the Tauride Palace was sealed
and guarded by a patrol with machine guns . . . Thus ended Russia's
first and last democratic parliament.

V. Chernov, 'Russia's One Day Parliament' from *The New Leader*
(31 January 1948)

After meeting for 12 hours, the Constituent Assembly was destined never
to meet again. Lenin had decided in advance that the Assembly would be
tested. If it endorsed the Bolsheviks' 'Declaration of Rights of the Toiling
and Exploited Peoples' which stated that 'the Constituent Assembly
unreservedly rallies to the policy of the Soviet authorities and feels that it
would be quite wrong, even technically, to set itself up in opposition to
. . . that power' (i.e. if it supported Soviet power) then it could be allowed
to proceed. The Assembly rejected the Bolshevik motion (by 237 votes to
138) but did not put forward an alternative form of government to the
Soviets.

In the early hours of the morning of 19 January the Bolsheviks walked
out, followed an hour later by the Left SRs. The former had already

planned to take their motion to the Third All-Russian Congress of Soviets. This had been called to coincide with the Constituent Assembly so that the legitimacy of Soviet power could be confirmed. This was even more certain since the peasants had by now swept the Left SRs to a massive majority in the Peasant Soviets (elected in December). Lenin justified the Bolsheviks' actions in the 'Decree on the Dissolution of the Constituent Assembly'.

4.7 Decree of the All-Russian Executive Committee of the Soviets on the dissolution of the Constituent Assembly (19 January 1918), drafted by Lenin and accepted by the Soviet

The Constituent Assembly, elected on the basis of lists drawn up before the October Revolution, was expressive of the old correlation of political forces, when the conciliators and the Constitutional-Democrats were in power.

Voting at that time for candidates of the Socialist-Revolutionary   5
Party, the people were not in a position to choose between the Right-Wing Socialist Revolutionaries, supporters of the bourgeoisie, and the Left-Wing Socialist Revolutionaries, supporters of Socialism. Thus the Constituent Assembly, which was to have crowned the bourgeois parliamentary republic, was bound to stand in the way of the October   10
Revolution and Soviet power . . .

Any renunciation of the sovereign power of the Soviets, of the Soviet Republic won by the people, in favour of bourgeois parliamentarism and the Constituent Assembly would now be a step backwards and would cause a collapse of the entire October Workers' and   15
Peasants' Revolution.

By virtue of generally known circumstances, the Constituent Assembly, opening on January 5 [18 January in the new calendar], gave the majority to the Party of the Right-Wing Socialist Revolutionaries, the party of Kerenksy, Avsentyev and Chernov. Naturally,   20
this party refused to discuss the absolutely precise, clear–cut and unambiguous proposal of the supreme body of the Soviet power, the Central Executive Committee of the Soviets, to recognise the programme of Soviet power, to recognise the Declaration of Rights of the Working and Exploited People, to recognise the October Revolu-   25
tion and Soviet power. By doing so the Constituent Assembly severed all ties with the Soviet Republic of Russia. The withdrawal from such a Constituent Assembly of the groups of Bolsheviks and Left-Wing Socialist-Revolutionaries, who are now in an indisputably vast major-

ity in the Soviets and enjoy the confidence of the workers and the   30
majority of the peasants, was inevitable . . .
        The Constituent Assembly is hereby dissolved.

Y. Akhapkin (ed.), *First Decrees of Soviet Power,* **1970**

Questions

1   From the tables in **4.5(b)** and **4.5(a)** can any deductions be made
     about the origins and nature of the support for the Bolsheviks, the
     Kadets and the Right SRs? In which particular group did Bolshevik
     slogans have their greatest impact?
2   Account for the fate of the Menshevik vote in **4.5(a)** and **4.5(b).**
3   Is there any evidence in **4.5(b)** to show that the Bolsheviks were
     unwise to hold the Constituent Assembly elections in November
     1917? What advice would you have given Lenin on this question?
4   List the reasons which the Soviet Executive Committee [**4.7**] gave for
     the dissolution of the Constituent Assembly. How convincing are they?
5   'Little that was said had any relation to the world outside.' How valid
     was E. H. Carr's verdict on the Constituent Assembly?
6   'The only real issue that was at stake in January 1918 was that of
     dictatorship versus democracy.' Discuss the truth of this statement.

The Terror

As in previous revolutions (e.g. revolutionary France between 1793 and
1794) the civil war which followed was to exacerbate greatly the conflict
between the rival parties. Once the Treaty of Brest-Litovsk had been
signed (see Chapter 5) the civil war intensified. The Left SRs abandoned
the government, not before returning to the traditions of the Right SRs in
assassinating leading Bolsheviks as well as the German ambassador.
With the intensification of the civil war came the intensification of the
Terror. Terror, in such circumstances, was not just a question of political
action to intimidate enemies but also a policy for transforming society.

4.8(a)   Lenin on the Terror in November 1917

We are accused of making arrests. Indeed, we have made arrests;
today we arrested the director of the State Bank. We are accused of
resorting to terrorism, but we have not resorted and I hope will not
resort, to the terrorism of the French revolutionaries who guillotined
unarmed men. I hope we shall not resort to it because we have   5

strength on our side. When we arrested anyone we told him we would let him go if he gave us a written promise not to engage in sabotage. Such written promises have been given.

V. I. Lenin, *Collected Works*, vol. 26, 1960

4.8(b) Trotsky speaking to the Petrograd Soviet on the officer cadet uprising (11 November 1917)

In Petrograd we won easily, thanks to propaganda ... We must bear in mind, however, that ... the dominant classes ... never relinquish their power without a bitter struggle. They have already begun to gather their forces, and are assuming the offensive ...
 ... We had to take decisive steps ... the Pavlovsky Cadet School is   5
destroyed ... We hold the cadets as prisoners and hostages. If our men fall into the hands of the enemy, let him know that for every worker and for every soldier we shall demand five cadets. We have demonstrated today that we are not joking ... They thought that we would be passive but we showed them that we can be merciless when   10
it is a question of holding on to the conquests of the revolution ...

From *Izvestia* no. 211 (12 November 1917) in J. Bunyan and
H. H. Fisher, *The Bolshevik Revolution 1917–1918*, 1934

4.8(c) Trotsky on the banning of the Kadet Party and the arrest of some of its members in December 1917

You protest against the mild terror which we are directing against our class enemies. But you should know that, not later than a month from now, the Terror will assume very violent forms after the example of the great French revolutionaries. The guillotine will be ready for enemies and not merely the jail.   5

Quoted in the SR newspaper *Delo Naroda* no. 223 (16 December 1917)
and reprinted in J. Bunyan and H. H. Fisher, *The Bolshevik
Revolution 1917–1918*, 1934

4.9 The Decree on the Judicature sets up revolutionary tribunals (5 December 1917)

In order to fight the counter-revolutionary forces and to protect the revolution and its gains against them, and also for the purpose of trying cases of marauding and pillage and the sabotage and misdeeds of merchants, industrialists, officials and other persons, worker-and-

peasant revolutionary tribunals shall be instituted consisting of a   5
chairman and six alternate assessors elected by the Gubernia [pro-
vince] or city Soviets of Workers', Soldiers' and Peasants' Deputies.

Special investigation commissions shall be instituted by the same
Soviets to conduct preliminary inquiry into such cases.

Chairman of the Council of People's Commissars, V. Ulyanov   10
(Lenin) Commissar: A. Shlikter, A. Shlyapnikov, J. Djugashvili
(Stalin), N. Avilov (N. Glebov), P. Stuchka

Y. Akhapkin (ed.), *First Decrees of Soviet Power*, 1970

4.10   A French diplomat in Moscow gives an impression of the effect the terror had on the Russian bourgeoisie and aristocracy

Friday 8 February 1918

We are living in a madhouse, and in the last few days there has been
an avalanche of decrees ... First comes a decree cancelling all banking transactions, then comes another one confiscating houses. A law is
being made to take away even their children from the bourgeois: from   5
the age of three they will be brought up in establishments where their
parents will always be able to go and see them a certain number of
times in the year. In this way, differences in education, which are
contrary to the sacred dogma of equality will be avoided, by degrad-
ing them all to the same level, that is to say the lowest level of all.   10

I have made no mention yet of the taxes which continue to hit
people from whom all source of income has been removed: five
hundred roubles for a servant, five hundred roubles for a bathroom,
six hundred roubles for a dog, and as much for a piano.

All inhabitants under the age of fifty are forced to join the 'per-   15
sonal labour corps'. Princess Obolensky has been ordered to go and
clear snow off the Fontanka Quay. Others have to sweep the tram-
lines at night.

From Louis de Robien, *The Diary of a Diplomat in Russia 1917–18*,
1969, quoted in J. Robottom, *Russia in Change*, 1984

4.11(a)   The Bolshevik, Dzerzhinsky, on the role of the Cheka, July 1918

The Cheka is not a court. The Cheka is THE DEFENCE OF THE
REVOLUTION as the Red Army is; as in the civil war the Red
Army cannot stop to ask whether it may harm particular individuals,

but must take into account only one thing, the victory of the revolution over the bourgeoisie, so the Cheka must defend the revolution   10
and conquer the enemy even if its sword falls occasionally on the heads of the innocent.

From E. H. Carr, *The Bolshevik Revolution*, 1973, vol. 1

4.11(b)   Lenin on the use of terror in March 1919

Very frequent changes are required of us in our line of conduct, which for the superficial observer may seem strange and incomprehensible. 'What's this?' he will say. 'Yesterday you were making promises to the petty bourgeoisie, and today Dzerzhinsky declares that Left SRs and Mensheviks will be put against the wall. What a   5
contradiction!' Yes, a contradiction. But there is also a contradiction in the behaviour of this same petty bourgeois democracy which does not know where to sit down, tries to sit between two stools, jumps from one to the other and falls over, now to the right, now to the left ... We say to it: 'You are not a serious enemy. Our enemy is the   10
bourgeoisie. But if you march with it, we shall have to apply to you too the measures of the proletarian dictatorship.'

From E. H. Carr, *The Bolshevik Revolution*, 1973, vol. 1

Questions

1   Why does **4.9** appear to make the setting up of the Cheka unnecessary? What does this appear to demonstrate about the situation of the Soviet Government in late 1918?

2   Account for the difference in tone between Lenin and Trotsky over the issue of terror [**4.8(a)–(c)**].

3   What was the aim of the policies of the Soviet Government described in **4.10**?

4   What does Lenin mean by the 'petty bourgeois democracy' [**4.11(b), line 7**]?

5   By using **4.8** to **4.11** trace the development of the Red Terror between 1917 and 1920? What factors could account for the systematic use of terror?

6   Compare **4.8(c)**, **4.9** and **4.10**. How would you evaluate their relative advantages and disadvantages as sources?

7   How far was the Bolshevik use of terror justified in the circumstances of the period 1917–21?

5 From world war to civil war

The Treaty of Brest-Litovsk, 1918

Historians of all shades of opinion agree that the key to Bolshevik victory in 1917 lay in their promise of immediate peace. The Decree on Peace [5.1] was the first act of the new Soviet Government. However, calling for peace and achieving it was not the same thing. Once the rapacity of German military demands became known, the Bolshevik Party split into three factions. The faction for accepting peace at any price, led by Lenin, was initially the smallest. It was only by doing a deal with Trotsky that Lenin was able to get the Party to accept the peace.

5.1 Proclamation to the Peoples and Governments of all the Belligerent Nations (The Decree on Peace), issued by the Second All-Russian Congress of Soviets (8 November 1917)

> The Workers' and Peasants' Government, created by the revolution of October 24–25 [November 6–7] and basing itself on the Soviets of Workers', Soldiers' and Peasants' Deputies, calls upon all the belligerent peoples and their governments to start immediate negotiations for a just, democratic peace. 5
>
> ... By such a peace the government means an immediate peace without annexation (i.e. without the seizure of foreign lands, without the forcible incorporation of foreign nations) and without indemnities ...
>
> The Government abolishes secret diplomacy, and for its part, announces its firm intention to conduct all negotiations quite openly 10 in full view of the whole people ...
>
> The Government proposes an immediate armistice to the governments and peoples of all the belligerent countries ... for a period of not less than three months ...
>
> While addressing the proposal of peace to the governments and 15 peoples of all the belligerent countries, the Provisional Workers' and Peasants' Government of Russia appeals in particular also to the class-conscious workers of the three most advanced nations of mankind and

the largest states participating in the present war, namely Great
Britain, France and Germany ... The workers of the countries   20
mentioned will understand the duty that now faces them of saving
mankind from the horrors of war and its consequences, that these
workers, by comprehensive, determined and supremely vigorous
action, will help us to conclude peace successfully, and at the same
time, emancipate the labouring and exploited masses of our population 25
from all forms of slavery and all forms of exploitation.

Chairman of the Council of People's Commissars
Vladimir Ulyanov-Lenin

From Y. Akhapkin (ed.), *First Decrees of Soviet Power,* **1970**

Questions

1   Compare the above Decree [5.1] with the Petrograd Soviet's 'Appeal
     to the Peoples of the World' of March 1917 [2.4]. What were the
     similarities and differences between them in regard to the ending of
     the war and which do you think the more effective to achieve that
     end? Give reasons for your choice.

2   In what ways did the Decree on Peace mark a 'revolution' in pre-
     viously accepted diplomatic procedures? How far do you think this
     contributed to the British and French governments' refusal to recog-
     nise the Bolshevik Government?

3   Compare a copy of President Wilson's *Fourteen Points of January,
     1958* (a brief summary putting them in context can be found in
     James Joll, *Europe Since 1870*, p. 234 or David Thomson, *Europe
     Since Napoleon*, pp. 571–2 – both currently available as Pelican paper-
     backs), with **5.1** above. What does this suggest about the impact of
     the October Revolution beyond the boundaries of Russia?

**5.2(a)   Lenin sets out the arguments for immediate acceptance of
German peace terms inside the Bolshevik Central Committee on
24 January 1918**

It is now a question of how we must defend the homeland – the
socialist republic. The army is utterly exhausted by war ... the
German position on the Baltic islands is so good that if they attacked
they could take Reval and Petrograd with their bare hands. If we
continue war in conditions like this, we will strengthen German   5
imperialism enormously and will have to make peace all the same, but

the peace will be worse then because we will not be the ones to
conclude it. There is no doubt that it is a shameful peace which we
are forced to conclude now, but if we embark on a war, our government will be swept away and another government will make peace.   10
Now we not only have the support of the proletariat but of the poor
peasants, too, and that will leave us if we continue the war. It is in
the interests of French, English and American imperialism to drag
out the war ... Those who advocate a revolutionary war point out
that this will involve us in a civil war with German imperialism and   15
in this way we will awaken revolution in Germany. But Germany is
only just pregnant with revolution and we have already given birth to
a completely healthy child, a socialist republic which we may kill if
we start a war ...

What comrade Trotsky suggests – halting the war, refusing to sign   20
a peace and demobilising the army – this is international political
showmanship. The only thing we will achieve by withdrawing our
troops is that we will give the Estonian socialist republic to the
Germans. It is said that if we conclude peace we will untie the hands
of the Japanese and the Americans, who will immediately take pos-   25
session of Vladivostok. But before they have reached Irkutsk, we will
have been able to make our socialist republic strong.

By signing peace, we will, of course, be handing over independent
Poland but we will keep the socialist Estonian republic and get a
chance to consolidate what we have won. If the Germans start to   30
attack, we will be forced to sign any peace at all and then, of course,
it will be a worse one. To save the socialist republic, reparation of
three milliards is not too high a price.

From A. Bone (ed.), *The Bolsheviks and the October Revolution*, 1974

**5.2(b)   Trotsky was not the most radical opponent of Lenin over
Brest-Litovsk. The Left Communists opposed peace on the grounds
that it would hold up the world revolution, and especially the
German revolution. They put forward another solution as outlined
here by Bukharin.**

Comrade Lenin has chosen to define revolutionary war exclusively as
a war of large armies with defeats in accordance with all the rules of
military science. We propose that war from our side – at least to start
with – will inevitably be a partisan war of flying detachments ... In
the very process of the struggle ... more and more of the masses will   5

gradually be drawn over to our side, while in the imperialist camp, on
the contrary, there will be ever increasing elements of disintegration.
The peasants will be drawn into the struggle when they hear, see and
know that their land, boots and grain are being taken from them –
this is the only real perspective.   10

From Geoffrey Hosking, *A History of the Soviet Union*, 1985

5.3   The effect the prospect of peace had on the Bolshevik supporters in the war ministry

February 1918. I remember how, late one night, we received from
our peace delegation at Brest-Litovsk a telegram which was rather
unclear. The gist of it was that the negotiations with Germany had
ended, the war was over, and our delegation was returning to Petrograd. All the officials of the commissariat who were present under-   5
stood the telegram to mean that peace had been signed. I remember
the joy and exultation that filled us all at that moment.

What, then, was our disappointment and chagrin when, towards
morning, we learnt from fresh telegrams that reached us that peace
had not been signed at all – that the negotiations had been broken off   10
by the chairman of the Soviet peace delegation, L. D. Trotsky, who
proclaimed the formula; 'neither peace nor war.' Our rejoicing had
been premature. Everyone appreciated that Trotsky was staking
everything on one card. His calculation was that the Germans would
be unable to advance against the Soviet republic.   15

Several days passed in agonised waiting. Each day that went by
peacefully instilled fresh hope. Why were the Germans not advancing? Perhaps the revolutionary infection really had penetrated so
deeply into the German Army that the soldiers were refusing to take
up arms against the red banners of the revolution? In that case   20
Trotsky had calculated correctly when he made his 'beau geste'.
Then, suddenly, as though out of a clear sky, came the thunderclap.
The Germans started to advance, and pressed with incredible speed
towards Petrograd.

I shall never forget the heavy, oppressive mood that then came   25
over our people in the Party and the Soviets. After a series of
uninterrupted successes, a blow like this, threatening to reduce to
naught all the conquests of the revolution! It seemed to many that all
was now lost, that we were going to be crushed by the armed might
of German imperialism, and the Soviet Republic was doomed to be   30

made a German colony. The first person who fell victim to this mood was my wife. After suffering torment for a whole day through her anxiety over the fate of the revolution and the Soviet Republic, in the evening of February 20 [new calendar] she shot herself.

From A. F. Ilyin-Zhenevsky (who worked at the Commissariat of War), *The Bolsheviks in Power: Reminiscences of the Year 1918,* **1984**

5.4(a)   The key military and territorial terms of the Treaty of Brest-Litovsk (signed on 3 March 1918)

[Article V]

Russia will, without delay, carry out the full demobilisation of her army inclusive of those units recently organised by the present government . . .

[Article VI]   5

Russia obligates herself to conclude peace at once with the Ukrainian People's Republic and to recognise the treaty of peace between that State and the Powers of the Quadruple Alliance. The Ukrainian territory will, without delay, be cleared of Russian troops and the Russian Red Guard. Russia is to put an end to all agitation or   10 propaganda against the Government or the public institutions of the Ukrainian People's Republic.

Estonia and Livonia will likewise, without delay, be cleared of Russian troops and the Russian Red Guard. The eastern boundary of Estonia runs, in general, along the river Narva. The eastern boundary   15 of Livonia crosses, in general, lakes Peipus and Pskov, to the south-western corner of the latter, then across Lake Luban in the direction of Livenhof on the Dvina. Estonia and Livonia will be occupied by a German police force until security is ensured by proper national institutions and until public order has been established. Russia will   20 liberate at once all arrested or deported inhabitants of Estonia and Livonia, and ensure the safe return of all deported Estonians and Livonians.

Finland and the Aaland Islands will immediately be cleared of all Russian troops and the Russian Red Guard, and the Finnish ports of   25 the Russian fleet and of Russian naval forces . . . Russia is to put an end to all agitation or propaganda against the Government or the public institutions of Finland.

From J. W. Wheeler-Bennett, *Brest-Litovsk: The Forgotten Peace, March 1918,* **1966**

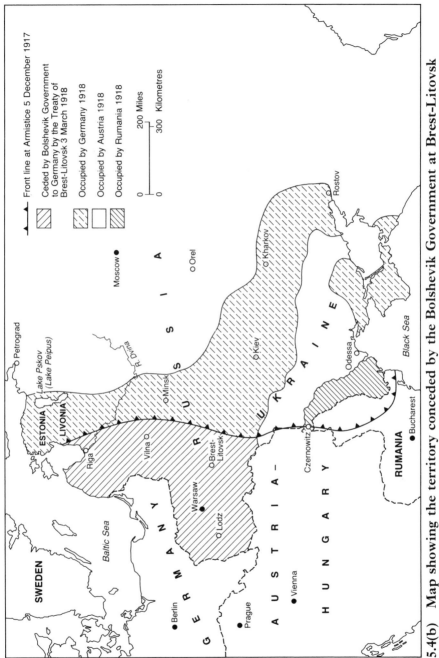

5.4(b) Map showing the territory conceded by the Bolshevik Government at Brest-Litovsk

Front line at Armistice 5 December 1917

Ceded by Bolshevik Government
to Germany by the Treaty of
Brest-Litovsk 3 March 1918

Occupied by Germany 1918

Occupied by Austria 1918

Occupied by Rumania 1918

200 Miles

300 Kilometres

Questions

1   What did Lenin mean when he stated that Germany was 'only just pregnant with revolution' [5.2(a), **line 17**]?
2   Summarise the three positions put forward by Lenin [5.2(a)], Trotsky (as summarised by Ilyin-Zhenevsky) [5.3], and the Left Communists [5.2(b)]. Discuss the similarities and differences of the arguments behind each of their positions.
3   How far does the evidence of Ilyin-Zhenevsky [5.3] support Lenin's verdict on Trotsky's 'international political showmanship' [5.2(a), **lines 21–22**]?
4   What light does Ilyin-Zhenevsky's evidence [5.3] throw on the Bolshevik Party's initial support for the position of the Left Communists [5.2(b)]?
5   Compare Lenin's fears in 5.2(a) with what actually happened at Brest-Litovsk [5.4(a) and 5.4(b)]. How much did the Bolsheviks actually lose by not signing the peace in January 1918?
6   Discuss the advantages and disadvantages as historical evidence of:
     (i) political speeches [5.2(a) and 5.2(b)]
     (ii) personal reminiscences [5.3]
     (iii) a legal document [5.4(a)]
     (iv) a map [5.4(b)]
7   'The Treaty of Brest-Litovsk was the logical culmination of Lenin's tactics for seizure of power' (Leonard Schapiro, *The Communist Party of the Soviet Union*, 1963). How fair is this as a judgement of the Bolsheviks at this time?
8   Statesman or political schemer. How do events surrounding Brest-Litovsk affect your judgement of Lenin?

The civil war 1918–20

With the signing of Brest-Litovsk the feeble opposition of ex-Tsarist generals was replaced by a more serious type of civil war. 'White' governments backed by the Entente powers, Britain, France and the United States, sprang up.

The civil war also markedly changed the political direction of the revolution. From this time forward the power of the Soviets declined, Soviet congresses, of which there were three in the first six months of the Bolshevik Government, became annual. The Soviet Executive Committee failed to act as a check on the Council of People's Commissars, which took all the important decisions. The basic Soviet principle of instant recall of delegates was abandoned in favour of formal elections but even these were not held as the civil war continued.

Gradually a new state power, not greatly dissimilar from that which the Bolsheviks had tried to destroy, began to appear. Having started with no police and no armies, and having abolished the death penalty, the Bolsheviks were forced to re-think their situation. From January 1918 they decreed the existence of a Red Army. In June 1918 the first death sentence against a 'counter-revolutionary' was carried out. By December 1920 the last White Army (that of Denikin in the Crimea) had been driven from Russian soil. The Bolsheviks had won the military campaign but there had been no world revolution. The documents 5.5–5.9 show how the Bolsheviks organised the Red Army and how fiercely the Civil War was fought.

5.5 The Decree of the Council of People's Commissars on the organisation of the Workers' and Peasants' Red Army (28 January 1915)

The old army was an instrument of class oppression of the working people by the bourgeoisie. With the transition of power to the work-ing and exploited classes there has arisen the need for a new army as the mainstay of Soviet power at present and the basis for replacing the regular army by the arming of the whole people in the near   5
future, and as a support for the coming socialist revolution in Europe.

[I]

In view of the aforesaid, the Council of People's Commissars resolves to organise a new army, to be called the Workers' and Peasants' Red Army, on the following principles: 10
(1) The Workers' and Peasants' Red Army is built up from the most conscious and organised elements of the working people.
(2) Access to its ranks is open to all citizens of the Russian republic who have attained the age of 18. Everyone who is prepared to devote his forces, his life to the defence of the gains of the October Revolu-   15
tion, the power of the Soviets, and socialism can join the Red Army. Joining the ranks of the Red Army requires characteristics from army committees or democratic public organisations standing on the plat-form of Soviet power, Party or trade union organisations, or at least two members of these organisations. Joining by whole units calls for   20
mutual guarantee and a signed vote.

From Y. Akhapkin, *First Decrees of Soviet Power*, 1970

5.6   The use of ex-Tsarist officers in the Red Army in 1918

Our attention was soon taken up with a problem which was very
important and also very controversial at the time – the problem of
drawing military specialists into our work. Hitherto our military
institutions and, even more strictly, our actual military units, had been
headed by Communists. Military specialists, that is, former officers   5
and generals of the old army, if they were enlisted at all, served only
as assistants or advisers to some leading Communist. What now came
up was the question of conferring on military specialists not only
duties but also powers – under unremitting Communist supervision,
of course. This idea arose in Moscow, in the People's Commissariat   10
for Military Affairs, and to promote it in Petrograd, a number of
leading comrades were specially despatched from Moscow, among
them I. T. Smilga, who was a member of our Party's Central
Committee. The arrival of the comrades was highly opportune, as the
new way that the question of drawing the specialists into our work   15
was presented was encountering a certain amount of opposition in
Petrograd . . . Giving positions of command to military specialists
seemed to us a very risky step. The Miller case [where an agent of
the Whites had penetrated the People's Commissariat for Military
Affairs] was still very vivid in our memory. Of course, to some   20
extent, the possibility of treachery was guarded against by the system
of military commissars, who had to stand beside every commander
who was a military specialist, but – and here arose a very big 'but' . . .
according to the new proposal a commissar had no power to interfere
with a commander's orders, even if he considered them incorrect, and   25
could only appeal against them to a higher authority. This point
especially attracted our objections.
    'But what if a commander orders his unit to overthrow the Soviet
power? Won't the commissar have the power to countermand that
order?' I demanded excitedly. Smilga smiled enigmatically. 'Besides   30
the written law there is the unwritten law', he said, patting his
revolver.

A. F. Ilyin-Zhenevsky, *The Bolsheviks in Power: Reminiscences of the
Year 1918*, 1984

Questions

1   What reason does **5.5** give for the setting up of the Red Army? What other possible reasons does the document omit?
2   What indications are there [**5.5**] that the idea of a permanent professional army was only temporary? Why do you think such an idea was important to the Bolsheviks in January 1918?
3   What was the significance of the Red Army's description as a 'Workers' and Peasants' Red Army' [**5.5, lines 8–9**]?
4   The members of which parties were eligible to volunteer for the Red Army in January 1918?
5   What was the function of a political commissar [**5.6**]?
6   In what kind of spirit and with what attitude do the Bolsheviks carry out the policies outlined in **5.5** and **5.6**? Refer to the texts to illustrate your argument.
7   Which of these documents [**5.5** and **5.6**] tells you more about the situation of the Bolshevik Government in 1918? Explain your choice.
8   'The civil war forced the Bolsheviks to abandon utopianism for realism.' Discuss.

Besides the formal Red Army organised directly by the Communist Party (the Bolsheviks took the name Communist Party of the Soviet Union in March 1918) there were many irregular forces which fought alongside the Bolsheviks. The Moscow government did not always have much control over them but as none of these 'partisans' wanted a return to the old order they made common cause with the Communists against the Whites.

Boris Pasternak's novel was written in the 1950s but was not published in Russia until the Gorbachev era. This was apparently because it did not treat the civil war as a period of political heroism in the birth of the Soviet Republic. Pasternak himself was based in the Ural Mountains in the early 1920s and this is the setting of the passage below.

5.7   The origins of the partisans as described by Boris Pasternak, a Russian writer

> Liberius, Libby for short, grew up a bit wild but he had all sorts of unusual gifts. When the war came he was fifteen. He faked the date on his birth certificate and made off to the front as a volunteer. His mother, who was anyway delicate, couldn't stand the shock. She took to her bed and didn't get up again. She died the year before last, just 5
> before the revolution.

'At the end of the war Liberius came back as a hero with three
medals and, of course, he was a fully bolshevised delegate from the
front. Have you heard about the "Forest Brotherhood"?'

'No, I'm afraid not.'   10

'In that case there's no sense in telling you the story, half the point
is lost. And there isn't any point in your staring out of the window at
the highway either. What's so remarkable about the highway nowa-
days? The partisans. And what are the partisans? They are the back
bone of the revolutionary army in the civil war, a force which arose   15
out of the conjunction of two factors: on the one hand, the political
organisation which assumed the leadership of the revolution, and on
the other, the rank and file of the army who refused to obey the old
authorities once the war was lost. Out of these two things the partisan
army came into being. Most of them are middle peasants, but you   20
find all sorts of people – poor peasants, unfrocked monks, sons of
kulaks up in arms against their fathers. There are anarchist idealists,
people on the run without passports, and boys expelled from school
for having had affairs with women. And German and Austrian prisoners of war tempted by the promise of freedom and repatriation.   25
Well, one of the units of this great people's army is called the Forest
Brotherhood, and the Forest Brotherhood is commanded by Comrade
Forester and Comrade Forester is Libby, Liberius Avercievich . . .'

B. Pasternak, *Doctor Zhivago*, 1958

5.8   A White colonel describes the punishment of a village
(March 1918) accused of supporting the Reds

Having surrounded the village they placed the platoon in position,
cut off the ford with machine guns, fired a couple of volleys in the
direction of the village, and everybody there took to cover. Then the
mounted platoon entered the village, met the Bolshevik committee,
and put the members to death, after which it demanded the sur-   5
render of the murderers and the instigators in the torturing of the
four Shirvan [name of village] men . . . They were delivered to us and
executed on the spot. The two officers concealed by the people of
Vladimirovka were guides and witnesses. After the execution, the
houses of the culprits were burned and the whole male population   10
under forty five whipped soundly, the whipping being done by the
old men. The people of this village are so brutal that when these
officers had been arrested the Red Guard themselves were not

thinking of murdering them, but the peasants, their women and even children insistently demanded their death ... Then the population 15 was ordered to deliver without pay the best cattle, pigs, fowl, forage and bread for the whole detachment, as well as the best horses. All this they kept bringing over until nightfall ... 'An eye for an eye'. The whole village set up a howl ...

M. G. Drozdovsky, *Diary of Colonel Drozdovsky March–April 1918,* 1923, **translated in J. Bunyan and H. H. Fisher,** *The Bolshevik Revolution 1917–1918,* 1934

5.9

This picture appeared in V. Serge, *Year One of the Russian Revolution* (1972), with the caption ' "He who does not work, neither shall he eat": the ex-bourgeois at compulsory labour, 1918'

Questions

1 Compare and contrast **5.9** with **6.3(a)**. How far do they agree in both fact and opinion? Explain your response fully.

2 'It has been known since antiquity that class wars are the most frightful (V. Serge).' How far does the evidence of **5.7** and **5.8** support this contention? What truth is there in the assertion?

The turning point of the civil war came at Petrograd in the autumn of 1919. The following passages below are extracts taken from the memoirs (written in 1944–5) of an anarchist sympathiser of Russian parentage who had spent most of his life in France. He arrived in Russia in 1919 and decided to support the Bolsheviks who asked him to assist in the running of the newly formed Third International.

5.10(a)   The role of Trotsky in the civil war

The news from the other fronts [of the civil war] was so bad that Lenin was reluctant to sacrifice the last available forces in the defence of a doomed city. Trotsky thought otherwise; the *Politburo* entrusted him with the final initiative. He arrived at almost the last moment and his presence instantly changed the atmosphere at Smolny, as it   5 did when he visited headquarters and the Peter-Paul Fortress.

Trotsky arrived with a train, that famous train which had been speeding to and fro along the different fronts .. The train of the Revolutionary War Council's President contained excellent motor-cars, a liaison staff, a court of justice, a printing shop for propaganda,   10 sanitary squads, and specialists in engineering, provisioning, street-fighting, all bound together by friendship and trust, all kept to a strict, vigorous discipline by a leader they admired, all dressed in black leather, red stars on their peaked caps, all exhaling energy. It was a nucleus of resolute and efficiently serviced organizers, who   15 hastened wherever danger demanded their presence.

They took everything in hand, meticulously, passionately. It was magical. Trotsky kept saying, 'It is impossible for a little army of 15,000 ex-officers to master a working class capital of 700,000 inhabitants.' He had posters put up proclaiming that the city would 'defend   20 itself on its own ground', that from now on this was the best strategic method, that the small White army would be lost in the labyrinth of fortified streets and there meet its grave.

V. Serge, *Memoirs of a Revolutionary*, translated and edited by Peter Sedgwick, 1963

5.10(b)   The relief of Petrograd (October 1919)

Petrograd was saved on 21 October at the battle of Pulkovo heights, some ten miles south of the half-encircled city. Defeat was trans-

formed into a victory so complete that Yudenich's troops rolled back
in disorder towards the Estonian frontier. There the Estonians
blocked their path. The White army that had failed to capture   5
Petrograd perished miserably. About 300 workers who had hastened
from Schlusselburg had also blocked the Whites at one critical
moment, before being mown down by a body of officers who
marched into the fray as though on parade.

It was an extraordinary fact, and one that proves how deep-rooted   10
in its causes, both social and psychological (they amount to the same),
our resilience was . . .

The White disaster was the result of two cardinal errors: their
failure to have the intelligence and courage to carry out agrarian
reform in the territories they wrested from the Revolution, and their   15
reinstatement everywhere of the ancient trinity of generals, high
clergy, and landlords.

**Victor Serge, *Memoirs of a Revolutionary*, translated and edited by
Peter Sedgwick, 1963**

Questions

1   What kind of role must Liberius have played in the Revolution if he
    was 'a fully bolshevised delegate from the front' [**5.7, lines 8–9**]?
2   What does **5.7** tell us about the nature of the organisation of the Red
    Army?
3   Why do you think the people of the village were 'so brutal' towards
    the officers [**5.8, line 12**]?
4   Compare **5.8** with Victor Serge's explanation for the victory of the
    Bolsheviks in the civil war [**5.10(a)** and **5.10(b)**]. How convincing is
    Serge's explanation and does the evidence of **5.8** confirm or deny his
    explanation in any way?
5   What are the particular strengths and weaknesses of literary sources
    like **5.8** to the historian?
6   How far do **5.8** to **5.10** help us to understand the ferocity with which
    the civil war was fought?
7   'It was the failings of the Whites rather than the strengths of the
    Bolsheviks that determined the outcome of the civil war.' How far is
    this an accurate verdict on the struggle between 1918 and 1921?

6 The economic consequences of the October Revolution

Bolshevik economic policies can be divided into three distinct stages. For the first six months they seemed to have thought only of administering capitalism. Grassroots action by workers and the realities of a bank strike and withdrawal of investment by industrialists led them to carry out various measures of socialisation. Once the civil war began and the economic and military problems began to accumulate, the Bolsheviks were forced to adopt more draconian measures which have since gone under the heading of 'war communism'. By 1921, with the civil war won but the country facing one of the worst famines in history, Lenin himself introduced what was to become known as the New Economic Policy (NEP). This abandoned many of the policies of the 1918–21 period and re-established a free market, not only in food but in industrial goods as well. For Lenin, NEP was introduced only as a temporary 'retreat', until an international revolution came to the aid of the Russian workers' state.

The land question

The first question that needed immediate treatment was the question of land. As the Bolsheviks had promised to satisfy the land hunger of the peasants they had no hesitation in issuing a land decree which basically borrowed the agrarian policy of the SRs – a policy the SRs had signally failed to carry out when in power.

6.1 The Decree on Land, issued by the Second All-Russian Congress of Soviets (8 November 1917)

(1) Private ownership of land shall be abolished for ever ... All land ... shall become the property of the whole people, and pass into the use of those who cultivate it.

Persons who suffer by this property revolution shall be deemed to be entitled to public support only for the period necessary for adaptation to the new conditions of life ...

(6) The right to use the land shall be accorded to all citizens of the Russian State (without distinction of sex) desiring to cultivate it by their own labour, with the help of their families, or in partnership,

5

but only as long as they are able to cultivate it. The employment of   10
hired labour is not permitted.

In the event of the temporary physical disability of any member of
a village commune for a period of up to two years, the village
commune shall be obliged to assist him for this period by collectively
cultivating his land until he is able to work.   15

Peasants who, owing to old age or ill health, are permanently
disabled and unable to cultivate the land personally, shall lose their
rights to the use of it but, in return, shall receive a pension from the
State.

(7) Land tenure shall be on an equality basis ... There shall be   20
absolutely no restriction on the forms of land tenure – household,
farm, communal or co-operative, as shall be decided in each individual village and settlement.

From Y. Akhapkin (ed.), *First Decrees of Soviet Power*, 1970

6.2 Lenin's defence of Bolshevik land policy

Voices are being raised here that the decree itself and the Mandate
were drawn up by the Socialist-Revolutionaries. What of it? Does it
matter who drew them up? As a democratic government, we cannot
ignore the decision of the masses of the people, even though we may
disagree with it. In the fire of experience, applying the decree in   5
practice, by carrying it out locally, the peasants will themselves realise
where the truth lies. And even if the peasants continue to follow the
Socialist-Revolutionaries, even if they give this party a majority in the
Constituent Assembly, we shall still say: 'What of it?' Experience is
the best teacher and it will show who is right; let the peasants solve   10
this problem from one end, and we shall solve it from the other.

V. I. Lenin, *Collected Works*, vol. 26, 1960

Questions

1   Why would the majority of peasants have welcomed the decree on
Land [6.1]?

2   What criticism would richer peasants (kulaks) have made of the
Decree [6.1]? What were the grounds for such criticism?

3   How does Bolshevik policy towards the peasants [6.2] in the first six
months of the revolution compare with their ideas towards other
social groups and institutions (compare with [4.4] and [6.7])?

4   To what is Lenin referring when he states that 'we cannot ignore the decision of the masses of the people' [6.2, lines 3–4]? How might a Menshevik have replied to him? State clearly, with justifications, which of them you would have agreed with.

5   What different light do [6.1] and [6.2] throw upon Bolshevik policy towards the peasants in the early months of the Revolution?

6   If one of these documents [6.1 or 6.2] were to be lost to history, which one would you choose to be saved? Justify your choice.

7   Lenin admitted that the Bolshevik Land Decree was copied from the most revolutionary proposals that had appeared in SR newspapers. Account therefore for the collapse of the Bolshevik coalition with the Left SRs and for the total failure of the Right SRs to accept the October Revolution.

Food crisis

The poor harvest of 1917 led to famine in the winter of 1917–18. According to Marcel Liebman, 'most parts of Russia were receiving only 12 or 13 per cent of the amount of bread officially "provided for" by the food commissariat. In April this fell by half.' (M. Liebman, *Leninism under Lenin*, 1980).

6.3(a)   An English nurse, who had been attached to the Tsarist armies passing through Moscow, recorded her impressions of the winter of 1918

January

I have already been in Moscow for several days and am able to take stock of my surroundings! I found the city in the throes of winter and famine; nevertheless, I was welcomed with open arms by my good friends and am staying with them as a member of the family,   5
sharing their lot and partaking of their meagre rations. After due investigations, the Red commissioners agreed to give me a permit for my own rations. Two potatoes or one eighth of a pound of bread was the daily ration per head. We preferred the potatoes, for, washed and cooked, every bit of them could be eaten – that is when they were not   10
bad! Whereas the bread inevitably contained sawdust and other 'foreign bodies', calculated to augment the weight. The market places provided a convenient rendez-vous for the surreptitious exchange of family heirlooms for foodstuffs. But no treasure could buy salt; it had ceased to exist . . .   15

I was walking the other morning on one of the side-streets when I happened to see the lean horse of a droschki [horse drawn sleigh] fall dead. The driver pulled the harness clear and left it where it had fallen. Some time later I returned by the same street. The carcass of the horse was still there, but devoid of most of its flesh. Some of the   20 starving had seized the opportunity to cut away all the meat that they could.

From Florence Farmborough, *Nurse at the Russian Front: A Diary 1914–18,* 1974

6.3(b)   A representative of the French Government described the situation in Moscow in April 1918

In the districts away from the centre, frightful poverty prevails. There are epidemics of typhus, smallpox, children's diseases. Babies are dying en masse. Those one sees are weak, fleshless, pitiful creatures. In the working class quarters one too often passes poor, pale, thin mothers, sadly bearing in their arms, in a little coffin of silver   5 painted wood, looking like a cradle, the tiny lifeless body that a small quantity of bread or milk would have kept alive.

J. Sadoul, *Notes sur la révolution bolchévique,* 1919

Questions

1   What threats to the people of Moscow and the Soviet Government are expressed in **6.3(a)** and **6.3(b)**?
2   What does **6.3(a)** tell us about the status of money in 1918?
3   The writer of **6.3(a)** was anti-Bolshevik whilst Sadoul [**6.3(b)**] later became a Bolshevik sympathiser. In what ways does this affect our evaluation of their evidence, if at all?

The food crisis caused the Bolsheviks to reconsider their policy. Peasants may have been happy enough to gain legal rights to the land but they were not disposed to give up their meagre surpluses. The countryside, as E. H. Carr has put it, was in 'passive revolt against the towns' (*The Bolshevik Revolution,* vol. 2, 1972). Symptomatic of this were the 'bagmen' who brought illegal supplies to the towns and sold them at inflated prices. The Bolshevik government was convinced that hoarding of grain by kulaks, the richer peasant farmers, was taking place as a deliberate attempt to cause famine and bring down the Government. As a result it was decided first to send commissars into the rural areas to organise committees of poor peasants against the kulaks. These would, it was hoped, conduct a war on the hoarding of their more affluent neighbours. When this too failed to increase the food supplies of the towns, volunteer detachments were sent out to requisition food.

6.4(a)   The establishment of an All-Russian Council of Supply, as reported in Gorky's newspaper, *Novaya Zhizn* ('New Life') (no. 12, 31 January 1918)

On January 27 there was a meeting of the All-Russian Food Congress made up of representatives of Soviets of Workers', Soldiers' and Peasants' Deputies. On the 29th the People's Commissar of Food, Schlichter, made a speech . . . He pointed out that the government of the People's Commissars is not to blame for the disorganisation of the food supply . . ., the situation had been critical in Kerensky's day . . . Schlichter further stressed the difficulties which the Soviet Government had encountered on account of the . . . sabotage of higher officials . . .   5

Some way must be found to get food out of the village. Armed detachments should be sent to compel the peasants to give up grain. Force alone, however, will not accomplish much. An exchange of goods between the city and the country should be organised. The village should be supplied with agricultural machinery, manufactured goods, iron, etc. This can be done only if there is a monopoly of industry. Transportation must also be improved by repairing and acquiring new rolling stock and by finding a means of fighting the soldier mobs who crowd the trains and disorganise the service. Some of the men dressed as soldiers are mere speculators . . .   10

   15

From J. Bunyan and H. H. Fisher, *The Bolshevik Revolution 1917–1918*, 1934

6.4(b)   The criticism made by Gorky in the newspaper, *Novaya Zhizn* ('New Life'), of the Council of People's Commissars' food policy in February 1918

After two weeks of trial the Sovnarkom [Council of People's Commissars] . . . removed [Schlichter's organisation] . . . and appointed an

extraordinary commission with Trotsky at the head. This commission
was given unlimited power and was made up of nine members . . .

    This extraordinary commission had decided to . . . shoot the bag-   5
men. It is agreed that the bagmen are an evil . . . but they are the
result and not the cause of the famine . . . (Had the exchange between
city and village been well-organised there would be no place for the
bagmen, but for some reason or other this exchange is not effective.
The famine grows apace and millions will perish.)   10

From J. Bunyan and H. H. Fisher, *The Bolshevik Revolution*
1917–1918, **1934**

6.5(a)   The war in the countryside between the requisitioning squads and the peasantry in April 1918

News is arriving of the bread war which is now taking place in
Voronezh, Smolensk, Tambov, Riazan, Simbirsk, Kursk, Kharkov.
Ufa, Orenburg, and a number of other gubernias [provinces]. Armed
detachments of Red Guards and hired soldiers are roaming over
villages and hamlets in quest of bread, making searches, laying traps   5
with more or less success. Sometimes they return with bread; at other
times they come back carrying the dead bodies of their comrades who
fell in the fight with the peasants . . .

    Many of the villages are now well-armed, and seldom does a bread
expedition end without victims . . . At the first report of a requisition-   10
ing expedition the whole volost [rural district] is mobilised . . . and
comes to the defence of the neighbouring village.

Novaya Zhizn **(19 April 1918) in J. Bunyan and H. H. Fisher,**
The Bolshevik Revolution 1917–1918, **1934**

6.5(b)   Maxim Gorky (Russian writer) tells Victor Serge of the attacks on commissars in the countryside in 1919

Hunger was weakening the masses, and distorting the cerebral processes of the whole country. At present it was imperative to side with
the revolutionary regime, for fear of a rural counter-revolution which
would be no less than an outburst of savagery. Alexei Maximovich
spoke to me of strange tortures rediscovered for the benefit of 'Com-   5
missars' in remote country districts; such as pulling out the intestines

through an incision in the abdomen and coiling them slowly around a tree. He thought that the tradition of these tortures was kept up through the reading of THE GOLDEN LEGEND*.

* THE GOLDEN LEGEND was a thirteenth century 'Lives of the Saints'

V. Serge, *Memoirs of a Revolutionary*, translated and edited by Peter Sedgwick, 1963

6.6   Output and gross yield of grain in the USSR (in pre-17 September 1939 borders)

Years	Productivity per ha in quintals	Gross yield in million quintals	% of previous year's output
1913	8.1	765.0	
1909–13 (average per year	6.9	651.8	
1917	6.4	545.6	
1918	6.0	495.3	90.7
1919	6.2	504.5	102.0
1920	5.7	451.9	89.5
1921	7.6	362.6	80.3

V. P. Danilov, *Sovetskaia dokolkhoznaia derevniia Naselenie, zemlepol' zovanie, khoziaistvo*), Moscow, 1977

Questions

1   Outline Schlichter's defence of the Food Commissariat in 6.4(a). How accurate is it?

2   What does 6.4(a) reveal about the general problems facing the Bolsheviks in 1918?

3   Compare Bolshevik policy in 6.4(a) and 6.4(b) with Lenin's speech on the land decree [6.2]. How would you explain the apparent discrepancy?

4   What is the significance of the Bolshevik policy towards the 'bagmen' expressed in 6.4(b)?

5   Explain Gorky's remark that hunger was 'distorting the cerebral processes of the whole country' [**6.5(b), lines 1–2**].

6   In the light of the evidence of **6.4(a)**, **6.4(b)** and **6.5(a)** can we ignore the story of the treatment of the commissars in **6.5(b)** as just another war atrocity exaggeration so common in history?

7   Account for the apparent discrepancy in Gorky's views in **6.4(b)** and **6.5(b)**.

8   What light do **6.1** to **6.5** throw on the reasons for the Bolsheviks' ultimate victory over the Whites?

9   What is the importance of **6.6** in explaining why 'war communism' in the countryside continued so long and why ultimately it came to be abandoned?

10   'As a party of the urban working class the Bolsheviks' attack on the peasantry was a product of ideology rather than necessity.' Discuss this verdict on 'war communism' between 1918 and 1921.

Far from carrying out their socialist ideas, the Bolsheviks were very cautious about any steps towards the socialisation of industry. However, pressure from the working class and lack of co-operation from the capitalists soon forced their hand.

Nationalisation and industry

6.7   The Bolsheviks and the bankers. Lenin's explanation to the Soviet Executive (VTsIK) on the seizure of the banks (27 December 1917)

To effect control we invited them [to talk], the men who run the banks, and together with them we worked out measures, to which they agreed, so that they could receive advances under conditions of full control and accountability ... We wished to proceed along the path of agreement with the bankers, we gave them advances to finance industries, but they started sabotage on an unprecedented scale, and experience compelled us to establish control by other methods.   5

V. I. Lenin, *Collected Works*, vol. 26, 1960

6.8(a)   Nationalisation from the bottom up. An account by Gurevich, an official in the Supreme Council of National Economy in 1918.

> There existed in theory a plan for the nationalisation of production. It was supposed that those branches of production which had come under the control of a few large companies would be nationalised first of all; and that in other branches of production nationalisation was to take place only after compulsory trustification and other ... measures 5 leading to centralisation had been introduced. In practice, however, there was no system in carrying out these measures. Everyone who wished to 'nationalise' did so; local 'sovnarkhozes' [councils of national economy], 'ispolkoms' [executive committees], 'voenrevkoms' [military revolutionary committees], [and] even the Chekas ... Such 10 action was generally prompted by some kind of motive in each individual case and was not due to any kind of plan. Sometimes an 'ispolkom' became angry with the factory owner, sometimes a person's fancy was caught by the supply of fuel of a certain factory, sometimes a competing [factory owner] would pay a special visit to 15 the presidium of the gubernia 'sovnarkhoz', bringing the necessary presents ... A nationalised [enterprise] was first swept by a wave of looting on the part of the various local authorities; and it was only after a considerable interval that the Supreme Council of National Economy gained control ... of the enterprise, taking it over in an 20 already completely ruined state ...

> From J. Bunyan and H. H. Fisher, *The Bolshevik Revolution 1917–1918,* 1934

6.8(b)   The economist, Kritsman

> After the proletarian revolution had undergone a preparatory period of eight months, distinguished in the economic sphere by hesitation and indecision, it took the pressure of an increasingly savage war and of the pro-capitalist intervention by the Kaiser's Germany, which used the Peace of Brest-Litovsk for its own end, for the proletarian 5 government to proclaim the expropriation of the expropriators by nationalising large-scale industry with the decree of 26 June 1918.

> L. Kritsman, *The Heroic Period in the Great October Revolution,* 2nd ed., 1926, translated in V. Serge, *Year One of the Russian Revolution,* 1972

6.8(c)   A Soviet economist lists the basic stages of the State takeover of the economy

The expropriation of the capital of the State through the formation of the Council of People' Commissars on 8 November [26 October] 1917; the expropriation of agriculture (decree on the nationalisation of land, passed on the same day); the expropriation of finance capital (decree on the nationalisation of the banks, 1 December [14] 1917);   5
expropriation of transport capital (decree on the nationalisation of water transport, 12 January [25] 1918; the expropriation of credit and principally of foreign credit (decree on the cancelling of loan, 14 January [27] 1918); the expropriation of the capital of rich peasants (decree establishing the Kombedy, or Committee of Poor Peasant,   10
11 June 1918); and the expropriation of big industrial capital (decree on the nationalisation of large-scale industry, promulgated on 28 June 1918).

L. Kritsman, *The Heroic Period in the Great October Revolution,* **2nd ed., 1926, translated in V. Serge,** *Year One of the Russian Revolution,* **1972**

6.9   Lenin's speech at the Congress of Factory Committees (June 1918)

We have always said: the emancipation of the workers must be performed by the workers themselves. We have always said: they cannot be liberated from outside; they themselves must learn how to solve historical problems ... and the more difficult these problems are, the more we see that millions of men must take a part in solving   5
them.

You must thoroughly understand, delegates from the factory committees, that nobody is going to come and help you, that from other classes you can expect not assistants but enemies, that the Soviet government has no loyal intelligentsia at its service.   10

Remember that if you in your factory and works committees concern yourselves with the workers' purely technical or financial interests, the revolution will not be able to keep a single one of its gains ... Your factory committees must become the basic state nuclei of the ruling class ...   15

V. I. Lenin, *Collected Works,* **1966, vol. 27**

Questions

1   What kind of 'sabotage' was Lenin referring to in **6.7, line 6**?
2   How far were the Bolsheviks committed to the idea of nationalisation when they came to power [**6.7** and **6.8**]?
3   How far does Gurevich [**6.8(a)**] undermine Lenin's view of workers' control in **6.9**? Was Lenin a utopian? Justify your answer.
4   In what way does Kritsman's evidence in **6.8(c)** clarify what Lenin meant by 'control by other methods' [**6.7, lines 7–8**]?
5   Compare and contrast the respective accounts of Gurevich [**6.8(a)**] and Kritsman [**6.8(b)** and **6.8(c)**]. Is it possible to induce the basis for their differences?
6   If two members of the same political party cannot agree on a contemporary event, what hope is there for historians three quarters of a century later? Do historians hold any advantages over contemporaries?
7   'An extraordinary mess, with each factory operating anarchically' (Victor Serge). How accurate is the view in **6.8(a)** and **6.8(b)** that there was no coherent Bolshevik plan for industry in the first six months of the revolution?
8   The Bolsheviks continued the list of nationalisations given in **6.8(c)** to include domestic commerce, small-scale industry and the co-operatives. These all occurred in 1918. Why does Kritsman not include them in his 'heroic period of the Great October Revolution'?
9   It is often asserted by the opponents of the Bolsheviks (from anarchists to conservatives) that they only promoted 'workers' control' as a means to achieve power and abandoned it as soon as possible thereafter. Given that the economy was largely nationalised and centrally controlled by the beginning of 1919, is this a fair assertion?

6.10(a)   Industrial resources according to the newspaper of the Petrograd Soviet

'Until the war', Izvestia explained, 'Petrograd industries had cheap foreign coal ... It is not likely that they will again be able to secure such fuel very soon. Our transportation service is so broken down that supplying Petrograd with coal from the Donetz or using oil to run the industries is not to be thought of. Under the circumstances Petrograd industries are doomed.'   5

Quoted in J. Bunyan and H. H. Fisher, *The Bolshevik Revolution 1917–1918*, 1934

6.10(b)   De-industrialisation. An account by L. M. Kleinbort (a Soviet economist opposed to Kritsman)

The demobilisation had to be carried out under conditions of an ever growing process of disorganisation (of industry) ... The oil fields of Baku, Grozny, and Emba regions came to a standstill ... The coal fields were in the same condition ... The production of raw materials was in no better state. The cultivation of cotton in Turkestan fell to   5
from 10 to 15 per cent of 1917 ... It was transport, however, that underwent a most rapid process of disintegration. ... These conditions little favoured a transition to peace production ... (and in so far as the proletariat was concerned) it spelled unemployment and nothing more ...   10
At the works of Siemens and Halske, out of 1,200 men, there remained only 700, and later no more than 300. The Nevsky shipbuilding works also closed ... 10,000 men being dismissed. The Obukhov works ... closed down, due to lack of coal. All together, 14,000 men were dismissed ...   15
Moscow factories were using peat and wood fuel and were less dependent upon Donetz coal than were the Petrograd works. Even (in the Moscow region), however, the war industries were being closed down and all their workers dismissed. The metal workers were those who suffered most ... All together, 215,000 workers were discharged.   20
'A feeling of apprehension and sadness hovers over Moscow', wrote Vecherniaia Zvezda: 'all life seems to have stopped ...'

L. M. Kleinbort, *Istoriia bezrabotitsy v Rossii 1857–1919 (History of Unemployment in Russia)*, 1925, translated in J. Bunyan and H. H. Fisher, *The Bolshevik Revolution 1917–18*, 1934

6.11   Numbers in the industrial workforce 1917–21 (in Russia)

Date	Number of Workers
1917	3,024,000
1918	2,486,000
1919	2,035,000
1920–21	1,480,000
1922	1,243,000

From M. Leibman, *Leninism under Lenin*, 1975

6.12   Industrial output in the USSR 1921–5

Produce	Unit	1913	1921	1925	1925 as percentage of 1913
Coal	million tonnes	29.1	9.5	16.5	57
Oil	million tonnes	9.2	3.8	7.1	77
Peat	million tonnes	1.7	2.0	2.7	159
Pig iron	million tonnes	4.2	0.1	1.3	31
Steel	million tonnes	4.2	0.2	1.9	45
Rolled steel	million tonnes	3.5	0.2	1.4	40
Electrical energy	million kWh	1,945	520	2,925	150
Cement	million tonnes	1.5	0.06	0.9	60
Tractors	(no.)	–	–	600	–
Paper	million tonnes	0.2		0.2	107
Sugar	million tonnes	1.3	0.05	1.1	85
Fish	million tonnes	1.0	0.3	0.7	70
Leather shoes	thousand pairs	8.3	3.4	8.2	98.8
All heavy industry	million rubles	10,251		7,739	75.5

From V. T. Chuntulov, *Ekonomicheskaya Istoriya SSSR*, 1969 and
E. Yu. Lokshin, *Ocherk istorii promyshlennosti SSSR*, 1956, in
R. Munting, *The Economic Development of the USSR*, 1982

Questions

1   In what ways does **6.10(b)** provide an explanation for the figures in **6.11**?

2   Comment on the evidence provided by **6.10(a)** and **6.12**. How far was Russia's industrial performance a result of the policies of the Bolshevik Government?

3   Lenin in 1921, when introducing the New Economic Policy stated that 'a peculiar war communism ... was forced on us by extreme want, it was not, and could not be, a policy that corresponded to the economic tasks of the proletariat' (*The Tax in Kind*). How accurate was this assessment?

7 The decline of the revolution

Many writers have identified March 1921 as a turning point in the revolution. In that month the Kronstadt rebellion seemed to indicate how far the Bolshevik Party had become divorced from the class it claimed to represent. In the same month, at the Tenth Party Congress, Lenin announced the replacement of 'war communism' by a new economic policy which basically restored the free market. At the same time factions were formally banned in the Bolshevik Party (although they continued to appear right up until the victory of Stalin in 1928). On the international front the failure of the March Action in Germany, the last independent attempt by German Communists to make their own revolution, left the Russian communists isolated. How could they survive in a hostile capitalist world?

The problem did not have to be tackled by Lenin: he suffered a series of strokes which largely incapacitated him from the beginning of 1922. By the time of his death, in January 1924, the struggle for the succession was already underway.

From war communism to New Economic Policy

7.1 An English visitor, C. E. Bechhofer, describes the situation in Russia in 1921

> The refugees are clustering in a dense crowd in two parts of the
> town – in the square near the station and beside the steamer piers on
> the Volga ... There is one story common to all these hundreds of
> people. All through the summer they have watched the soil harden to
> stone under the rays of the terrible sun and the few scattered shoots   5
> which had pushed their heads through it blacken and perish. They
> had been living on the tiny remnants of the last year's harvest –
> which also, it must be remembered, was a failure – eked out with all
> kinds of surrogates – acorns, bark, lime-tree leaves, pigweed, clay,
> insects beaten up into a paste, even animals' droppings – anything   10
> that will hold a modicum of flour together and cheat them into
> imagining that they are eating something ... And all the time they
> grow thinner and thinner; and some of them die and the rest get

ready to follow them. In their faces is absolute despair . . . 'One of
my children died yesterday', says an old peasant, almost without   15
looking up at me, 'another died three days ago. We shall all die soon.'

C. E. Bechhofer, *Through Starving Russia*, 1921

7.2   Collecting the bodies of the victims of starvation, 1922

Hulton Picture Library

7.3   Lenin's criticism of 'war communism' (March 1921)

Lifted up on a wave of exaltation, and having behind us the general
political and later, the military enthusiasm of the people, we intended
on the basis of this enthusiasm to carry out . . . similarly exalted
economic tasks. We expected – or perhaps it would be more correct to
say that we assumed without sufficient calculations – that by the   5
direct fiat of the proletarian state we would be able to establish state
production and state distribution of products on a communistic basis
in a country of small peasants. Life has exposed our error. There was
a need of transition stages . . . The fundamental question, from the
point of view of strategy, is; Who will take sooner advantage of this   10
new situation? Who will win? The capitalist whom we are now letting
in through the door or even through several doors which we ourselves
ignore . . . or the sovereign power of the proletariat.

V. I. Lenin, *Collected Works*, vol. 32, 1960

7.4   Lenin justifies the New Economic Policy, April 1921

The civil war of 1918–20 greatly increased the devastation of the
country, retarded the restoration of its productive forces, and bled the
proletariat more than any other class. To this was added the failure of
the harvest of 1920, the fodder shortage, the dying off of cattle, which
still further retarded the restoration of transport and industry,   5
because, among other things, it interfered with the employment of
peasants' horses for carting wood, our main fuel . . .

We were forced to resort to 'War Communism' by war and ruin
. . . it was a temporary measure. We are still in such a state of ruin
. . . that we cannot give the peasant manufactured goods for ALL we   10
require. Knowing this we are introducing the tax in kind, i.e. we shall
take the minimum of grain we require (for the army and the workers)
in the form of a tax and will obtain the rest in exchange for manufactured goods . . . Our poverty and ruin are so great we cannot hope to
restore large-scale factory state socialist production at one stroke . . .   15

Hence, it is necessary, to a certain extent, to help to restore
SMALL industry . . . the effect will be the revival of the petty
bourgeoisie and of capitalism on the basis of a certain amount of free
trade. This is beyond doubt.

. . . The proletarian regime is in no danger as long as the   20
proletariat firmly hold power in its hands, as long as it firmly holds
transport and large-scale industry in its hands . . .

We must not be afraid of Communists 'learning' from bourgeois
specialists, including merchants, small capitalist co-operation and
capitalists.

V. I. Lenin, *Collected Works*, vol. 32, 1960

Questions

1   Examine the causes of the famine of 1921 as given in **7.1, 7.3** and **7.4**.
     Were the Bolsheviks unlucky or short-sighted? Justify your answer.
2   How, if at all, do **7.1** and **7.2** help our assessment of the evidence in
     7.3 and **7.4**?
3   Examine the contradictions between **7.3** and **7.4**. Do they invalidate
     political speeches as sources of historical evidence? Can they be
     understood or reconciled in any way? In each case explain your
     answer fully.

4   From the evidence of **7.4**, how far was the New Economic Policy a
     break with 'war communism'?

5   'A temporary retreat', 'An admission of failure'. Discuss these ver-
     dicts on the NEP examining the degree of truth contained in each.

Kronstadt

As the civil war drew to a close, the privations of the workers in
Petrograd led to a series of strikes at the beginning of 1921. Twenty five
miles away the sailors of the Kronstadt naval base mutinied in support of
the strikers. However, they also made political demands including the
need for new elections to the Soviet. A resolution passed aboard the
battleship 'Petropavlovsk' became the programme of the revolt.

7.5   The Petropavlovsk resolution which became the manifesto of the Kronstadt Revolt of March 1921

Having heard the report of the representatives of the crews sent by
the general meeting of ships' crews to Petrograd to investigate the
state of affairs there, we demand:
(1)   that in view of the fact that the present Soviets do not express
the will of the workers and peasants, new elections by secret ballot be   5
held immediately, with free preliminary propaganda for all workers
and peasants before the elections;
(2)   freedom of speech and press for workers and peasants, anarchists and left socialist parties;
(3)   freedom of assembly for trade unions and peasant associations;   10
(4)   that a non-party conference of workers, Red Army soldiers and
sailors of Petrograd, Kronstadt and Petrograd Province be convened
not later than 10th March 1921;
(5)   the liberation of all political prisoners of socialist parties, as well
as all workers and peasants, Red Army soldiers and sailors impri-   15
soned in connection with the working class and peasant movements;
(6)   the election of a commission to review the cases of those who
are held in jails and concentration camps;
(7)   the abolition of all political departments because no single party
should have special privileges in the propaganda of its ideas and   20
receive funds from the state for this purpose; instead of these departments, locally elected cultural-educational commissions should be
established, to be financed by the state;

(8)   that all roadblock detachments (to prevent food smuggling) be
removed immediately;   25
(9)   the equalisation of the rations of all toilers, with the exception of
those working in trades injurious to health;
(10)   the abolition of the Communist fighting detachments in all
military units, as well as various Communist guards kept on duty in
factories and plants; should such guards or detachments be needed,   30
they could be chosen from the companies in military units, and at the
discretion of the workers in factories and plants;
(11)   that the peasants be given the right and freedom of action to
do as they please with all the land and also the right to have cattle
which they themselves must maintain and manage, that is without the   35
use of hired labour;
(12)   we request all military units, as well as the comrades 'kursanty'
(military cadets) to endorse our resolution;
(13)   we demand that all resolutions be widely published in the
press;   40
(14)   we demand the appointment of a travelling bureau for control;
(15)   we demand that free handicraft production by one's own
labour be permitted.

Pravda o Kronshtadte

Victor Serge was an ex-anarchist who became a Bolshevik supporter
(see also **5.10(a)** and **5.10(b)**) but found it very difficult to decide which
side to support in March 1921. He was appalled by the way the
Communist government dealt with the rising.

7.6(a)   The lies of the press

The truth seeped through little by little, past the smokescreen put
out by the Press, which was positively berserk with lies. And this was
our own Press, the Press of our revolution, the first Socialist Press,
and hence the first incorruptible and unbiased Press in the world!
Before now it had employed a certain amount of demagoguery, which   5
was, however, passionately sincere, and some violent tactics towards
its adversaries. That might be fair enough and at any rate was
understandable. Now it lied systematically ... The Kronstadt insurrection had shed no single drop of blood, and merely arrested a few
Communist officials, who were treated absolutely correctly; the great   10

majority of Communists, numbering several hundreds, had rallied to
the uprising (a clear proof of the Party's instability at its base). All
the same the legend of narrowly averted executions was put around.
Throughout this tragedy, rumour played a fatal part. Since the
official Press concealed everything that was not a eulogy of the   15
regime's achievements, and the Cheka's doing was shrouded in utter
mystery, disastrous rumours were generated every minute. The
Kronstadt mutiny began as a movement of solidarity with the Petrograd strikes, and also as a result of the rumours, which were over-
whelmingly false, about their repression.   20

**V. Serge, *Memoirs of a Revolutionary*, translated and edited by Peter
Sedgwick, 1963**

In the end, Victor Serge sided with the government.

7.6(b)   Choosing sides in March 1921

After many hesitations, and with unutterable anguish, my Communist
friends and I finally declared ourselves on the side of the Party. This
is why. Kronstadt had right on its side. Kronstadt was the beginning
of a fresh, liberating revolution for popular democracy; 'The Third
Revolution!' it was called by certain anarchists whose heads were   5
stuffed with infantile illusions. However the country was absolutely
exhausted, and production practically at a standstill; there were no
reserves of any kind, not even reserves of stamina in the hearts of the
masses. The working class elite that had been moulded in the struggle against the old regime was literally decimated. The Party, swollen   10
by the influx of power seekers, inspired little confidence. Of the other
parties only minute nuclei existed, whose character was highly ques-
tionable . . .
    If the Bolshevik dictatorship fell, it was only a short step to chaos,
and through chaos to a peasant rising, the massacre of the Commu-   15
nists, the return of the emigrés, and, in the end, through sheer force
of events, another dictatorship, this time anti-proletarian.

**V. Serge, *Memoirs of a Revolutionary*, translated and edited by Peter
Sedgwick, 1963**

The Kronstadt revolt lasted from 28 February to 18 March 1921. During
that time there were some negotiations but there was little possibility of
agreement. The original attack began on 8 March, but the troops used

being unreliable, the Bolsheviks waited until they had brought up officer cadets of the Red Army and Cheka units. The second attack began on the night of 16 March, and by 18 March the entire city had been re-occupied. Over 300 Communist delegates from the Tenth Party Congress had joined in the assault on the fortress and 15 of them died. It is not known how many died altogether but the anarchist writer Paul Avrich estimates that the government side lost 10,000 whilst the defenders of Kronstadt lost 1,500 dead with 2,500 captured. (See *Kronstadt 1921*, 1970).

7.7(a)   The crushing of Kronstadt

Novosti

7.7(b)   The final defeat of Kronstadt

At the beginning of March, the Red Army began its attack, over the ice, against Kronstadt and the fleet. The artillery from the ships and forts opened fire on the attackers. In several places the ice cracked open under the feet of the infantry as it advanced, wave after wave, clad in white sheets. Huge ices-floes rolled over, bearing their human 5 cargo down into the black torrent. It was the beginning of a ghastly fratricide.

 . . . The business had to be got over before the thaw began. The final assault was unleashed by Tukhachevsky on 17 March, and culminated in a daring victory over the impediment of the ice.   10

Lacking any qualified officers, the Kronstadt sailors did not know
how to employ their artillery; there was, it was true, a former officer
named Kozlovsky among them, but he did little and exercised no
authority. Some of the rebels managed to reach Finland. Others put
up a furious resistance, fort to fort and street to street; they stood and   15
were shot crying 'Long live the world revolution!'. There were some
of them who died shouting, 'Long live the Communist International!'. Hundreds of prisoners were taken away to Petrograd and
handed to the Cheka; months later they were still being shot in small
batches, a senseless and criminal agony.   20

**V. Serge, *Memoirs of a Revolutionary*, translated and edited by Peter
Sedgwick, 1963**

Questions

1   It is often asserted that the basic demand of the Kronstadt revolt was
    for 'Soviets without Communists'. In the light of the evidence in **7.5**
    how true is this?
2   Examine the relationship between the economic demands of the
    Kronstadters [**7.5**] and the New Economic Policy [**7.4**]. Is there any
    truth in the view that the Kronstadt Revolt provoked the economic
    'retreat'?
3   In what ways does Serge's evidence [**7.6(a)** and **7.6(b)**] throw light on
    the reasons for the Kronstadt Revolt and the nature of the Bolshevik
    regime by March 1921?
4   Why had 'the business . . . to be got over before the thaw began'
    [**7.7(b), line 8**]?
5   **7.7(a)** adds little to our understanding of the Kronstadt events.
    Discuss.
6   Discuss the value of Serge's evidence on the Bolshevik revolution at
    this point.
7   'A tragic necessity' (Trotsky). How accurate a summary of the Kron-
    stadt Revolt is this?

7.8   Lenin on 'Kronstadt's Historical Place' (15 March 1921)

I believe that there are only two kinds of government possible in
Russia – a government by the Soviets or a government headed by a
tsar. Some fools or traitors in Kronstadt talked of a constituent
assembly, but does any man in his senses believe for a moment that a
constituent assembly at this critical abnormal stage would be anything   5

but a bear garden? This Kronstadt affair in itself is a petty incident. It no more threatens to break up the Soviet state than the Irish disorders are threatening to break up the British Empire.

Some people in America have come to think of the Bolsheviks as a small clique of very bad men who are tyrannizing over a vast number 10 of highly intellectual people who would form an admirable government among themselves the moment the Bolshevik regime was overthrown. This is a mistake, for there is nobody to take their place save butcher generals and helpless bureaucrats who have already displayed their total incapacity for rule. 15

If people abroad exaggerate the importance of the rising in Kronstadt and give it support, it is because the world has broken up into two camps: capitalism abroad and Communist Russia.

V. I. Lenin, *Collected Works*, 1966, vol. 36

Lenin's last years

A symptom of the Bolshevik failure to live up to their ideals was the growth of a series of internal oppositions inside the Communist Party. Although officially outlawed, these oppositions continued to exist and Lenin began to see that the real threat was not dissidence but bureaucracy.

7.9   The criticisms of the Workers' Opposition in March 1921

Taking into consideration the utter collapse of our industries while still clinging to the capitalist mode of production (payment for labour in money, variations in wages received according to the work done) our Party leaders, in a fit of distrust in the creative abilities of workers' collectives, are seeking salvation from the industrial chaos. 5 Where? In the hands of scions of the bourgeois–capitalist past. In businessmen and technicians, whose creative abilities in the sphere of industry are subject to the routine, habits and methods of the capitalist system of production and economy. They are the ones who introduce the ridiculously naive belief that it is possible to bring 10 about Communism by bureaucratic means . . .

There can be no self-activity without freedom of thought and opinion, for self activity manifests itself not only in initiative, action and work, but in independent thought as well. We give no freedom to class activity, we are afraid of criticism, we have ceased to rely on the 15 masses: hence we have bureaucracy with us . . .

The stronger the Soviet authority becomes, the greater is the
number of the middle class, and sometimes openly hostile elements,
joining the Party. The elimination of these elements must be complete and thorough ... The Workers' Opposition proposes to register   20
all members who are non-workers and who joined the Party since
1919, and to reserve for them the right to appeal within three months
from the decisions arrived at, in order that they might join the Party
again ...

... The Party must reverse its policy in relation to the elective   25
principle ... The practice of appointments completely rejects the
principle of collective work. It breeds irresponsibility. Appointments
by the leaders must be done away with and replaced by the elective
principle at every level of the Party. Candidates shall be eligible to
occupy responsible administrative positions only when they have been   30
elected by conferences or congresses.

**From *The Workers' Opposition*, the document presented by Alexandra
Kollontai to the Tenth Communist Party Congress. It was originally
printed in the Left Communist paper of Sylvia Pankhurst's *Workers'
Dreadnought* in 1921. These extracts are from the pamphlet *The
Workers' Opposition*, 1968**

7.10   The Preliminary Draft Resolution of the Tenth Congress of the Russian Communist Party on Party Unity (March 1921)

All class conscious workers must realise that factionalism of any kind
is harmful and impermissible, for no matter how members of individual groups may desire to safeguard Party unity, factionalism in
practice inevitably leads to the weakening of team-work and to intensified and repeated attempts by the enemies of the governing Party,   5
who have wormed their way into it, to widen the cleavage and use it
for counter-revolutionary purposes ...

... The Congress, therefore, hereby declares dissolved and orders
the immediate dissolution of all groups without exception formed on
the basis of one platform or another (such as the Workers' Opposition   10
group, the Democratic Centralism group, etc.). Non-observance of
this decision of the Congress shall entail unconditional and instant
expulsion from the Party.

V. I. Lenin, *Collected Works*, vol. 32, 1960

Questions

1   How accurate were Lenin's assessments of:
   (i) the political alternatives for Russia
   (ii) the significance of Kronstadt
   (iii) the state of the world
   in **7.8**?
2   Compare the analysis of the situation in Russia in 1921 made by Lenin [**7.3, 7.4, 7.8** and **7.10**] and the Workers' Opposition [**7.9**]. What were their respective positions on:
   (i) the road to socialism?
   (ii) the organisation of the economy?
   (iii) the nature of the state?
   (iv) the role of the party?
   How do you account for Lenin's rejection of the positions of the Workers' Opposition?
3   Compare Lenin's speech 'On Party Unity' [**7.10**] with his position in 1918 [**4.4**]. How do you explain the changes in his position?
4   'With the banning of factions in March 1921 the last bulwark against Party dictatorship was abolished.' How true is this statement?

The decline of the Bolshevik Party mirrored the decline of the original revolutionary working class of 1917. In October 1921 Lenin announced that 'The proletariat has disappeared'. In its place was a huge bureaucracy which had risen from 114,359 members in 1918 to nearly six million in 1920.

7.11   Lenin's words to the Eleventh Congress of the Russian Communist Party (March 1922) on bureaucracy

> ... and if we take that huge bureaucratic machine, that gigantic heap, we must ask: who is directing whom? I doubt very much whether it can be truthfully said that the Communists are directing that heap. To tell the truth they are not directing, they are being directed.

> **V. I. Lenin,** *Collected Works,* **1966, vol. 33**

7.12   Lenin's Testament (25 December 1922)

> ... Our Party rests upon two classes, and for that reason its instability is possible, and if there cannot exist an agreement between those classes its fall is inevitable. In such an event it would be useless to take any measures or in general to discuss the stability of our central

committee. In such an event no measures would prove capable of   5
preventing a split. But I trust that this is too remote a future, and too
improbable an event to talk about.

I have in mind stability as a guarantee against a split in the near
future . . .

I think that the fundamental factor in the matter of stability . . . is   10
such members of the central committee as Stalin and Trotsky. The
relation between them constitutes, in my opinion, a big half of the
danger of that split, which might be avoided, and the avoidance of
which might be promoted, in my opinion, by raising the number of
members of the central committee to fifty or one hundred.   15

Comrade Stalin, having become general secretary, has concentrated
an enormous power in his hands; and I am not sure that he always
knows how to use that power with sufficient caution. On the other
hand, comrade Trotsky . . . is distinguished not only by his excep-
tional abilities – personally he is, to be sure, the most able man in the   20
present central committee – but also by his too far-reaching self-
confidence and a disposition to be too much attracted by the purely
administrative side of affairs.

These two qualities of the two most able leaders of the present central
committee might, quite innocently, lead to a split; if our party does not   25
take measures to prevent it, a split might arise unexpectedly . . .

From E. H. Carr, *The Interregnum 1923–1924,* 1954

Questions

1   Examine **7.11** and **7.12**. How consistent are they in their analysis of
both the problems facing Russia after 1923 and their solutions?

2   Using the documents in Chapters Four to Seven draw up your own
timeline of the main events under the headings of political, economic
and social and international. Does this enable you to draw any
conclusions about the development of the revolution, and if so, what
are they?

3   In the light of the evidence of **7.11** and **7.12** how far is it possible to
believe that 'the dictatorship of the proletariat' still existed in Russia
at the death of Lenin?

4   How far does **7.12** provide evidence for the further decline of the
Bolshevik Party?

5   'Soviet democracy was the unfulfilled promise of the Russian Revolution.' Discuss.

Key personalities

Bukharin, Nikolai Ivanovich (1888–1938)

Joined the Bolsheviks as a result of the 1905 Revolution. The 'favourite of the Party' (Lenin), also one of its leading theoreticians. His *Imperialism and World Economy*, 1915, assisted Lenin's own formulations on imperialism in 1916. Led the Moscow Bolsheviks 1917–1918; resigned from the Party over the acceptance of the Treaty of Brest-Litovsk which he regarded as a betrayal of the international revolution. Moved further to the Right during the Civil War. Supporter of NEP and Stalin in the 1920s, wrote the Soviet Constitution in 1936, before being sentenced to death in the Moscow Show Trials. Rehabilitated in the USSR in 1988.

Chernov, Vladimir Mikhailovich (known as Victor) (1876–1952)

Began political activity in 1893, a founder of the Socialist-Revolutionary Party in 1903. Minister of Agriculture under Kerensky after July 1917, became leader of the Right SRs after the split in October 1917. President of the Constituent Assembly in January 1918, and played a leading role in the revolt of the Czechoslovak Legion in 1918. Wrote *The Great Russian Revolution* in exile in Western Europe and died in the USA.

Chkheidze, Nicholas Semyonovich (1864–1926)

Leader of the Mensheviks in the Third and Fourth Dumas (1907–17), he was also on the first Praesidium of the Petrograd Soviet when it was formed in March 1917. Replaced by Trotsky as Chairman of the Petrograd Soviet in September 1917. Went abroad after the October Revolution and committed suicide.

Dan (real name, Gurevich) Feodor Ilyich (1871–1947)

Menshevik leader who began political activity in 1896. A doctor, he became editor of *Izvestia* (the paper of the Petrograd Soviet) in 1917. Leader of one of the two factions of Menshevik Internationalists formed in 1918. Tried to act as an opposition to the Bolsheviks within Russia but eventually went into exile in 1922, and died in New York.

Dzerzhinsky, Felix (1877–1926)

Began political activity with the Social Democrats in 1895. After several spells in Siberia he joined the Bolshevik faction. Most renowned as the founder of the Cheka, the political police, in December 1918. Subsequently People's Commissar for Internal Affairs, then Communications, and finally President of the Supreme Economic Council of the USSR.

Gorky, Maxim (Alexei Maximovich Peshkov) (1868–1936)

Born in Nizhni Novgorod (now renamed after him), the leading Russian playwright and novelist of this century. Became a Menshevik Internationalist during the First World War. After the February Revolution he founded the newspaper *Novaya Zhizn* ('New Life') which attacked both Kerensky and the Bolsheviks (although he remained a lifelong friend of Lenin). A friend of Stalin, he defended the gains of the revolution until his mysterious death (for which his doctor was later hanged). Hailed as the 'father of Soviet literature' and given a state funeral by Stalin.

Guchkov, Alexander Ivanovich (1862–1936)

A wealthy Moscow capitalist, he became the leader of the Octobrist Party. In the process of trying to organise the palace revolution to overthrow Nicholas II when the February Revolution broke out. Became Minister of War and Navy in the first Provisional Government but resigned when his policy of war to victory was opposed by the Soviet. Supported the Whites in the Civil War before emigrating to Berlin in 1921.

Kamenev (Rosenfeld), Lev Borisovich (1883–1936)

Joined the Social Democratic movement in 1901 and a close ally of Lenin after the split with the Mensheviks in 1903. Opposed the April Theses and the October Revolution, but remained a member of the Central Committee of the Party until 1927. Formed a triumvirate with Zinoviev and Stalin to keep Trotsky out of power. Subsequently broke with Stalin to form the United Opposition with Trotsky. Shot after the Show Trials of 1936.

Kerensky, Alexander Fyodorovich (1881–1970)

A member of the Trudovik, or Labour group, on the right wing of the Socialist-Revolutionary Party. A staunch supporter of the war effort, he precipitated himself into a position of strength in the February Revolution by taking a post on the Praesidium of the Petrograd Soviet and, at the same time, becoming Minister of Justice in the Provisional Government. After the July Days he became Prime Minister until the October Revolution overthrew him. Noted for his flights of oratory which bordered on the hysterical, he retired to the USA.

Kolchak, Alexander Vasilievich (1873–1920)

Became admiral of the Black Sea Fleet in 1916 and resigned in July 1917. Became undisputed leader of the White forces beyond the Urals and declared himself Supreme Ruler of Russia in November 1918. Noted for shooting the SR government in Omsk, he was himself captured by Czechs in 1920 and handed over to the local revolutionary committee which had him shot.

Kollontai, Alexandra Mikhailovna (1873–1952)

Active in the Russian Social Democratic movement from 1896 she was a Menshevik until 1915. Elected to the Executive Committee of the Petrograd Soviet in March 1917. Arrested by the Provisional Government after the July Days. Opposed the Treaty of Brest-Litovsk but remained loyal to the Party. Drafted the Theses of the Workers' Opposition for the Tenth Party Congress in 1921 and after their defeat went in for a diplomatic career, mainly in Scandinavia.

Kornilov, Lavr Georgevich (1870–1918)

Tsarist General who was appointed Commander-in-Chief of the Russian Army by Kerensky in July 1917. Subsequently headed a revolt aimed at undermining working-class control of the revolution. May also have sought a military dictatorship. He escaped after the October Revolution and was killed fighting with the White armies on the Don.

Krupskaya, Nadezhda Konstantinova (1869–1939)

Co-worker and wife of Lenin, Secretary of the Bolshevik Committee Abroad whilst in exile, and holder of various government posts after 1917.

Lenin (Ulyanov), Vladimir Ilyich (1870–1924)

Founded the Combat Union for the Emancipation of the Working Class in St Petersburg with Martov in 1895 and was almost immediately arrested and sent to Siberia. Made a Marxist analysis of Russian economic development, *The Development of Capitalism in Russia*, in 1899. In 1903 he forced the split between Bolsheviks and Mensheviks in the recently formed Russian Social Democratic Party over the nature of the party and its membership. Spent most of the rest of his career in Swiss exile but arrived back in Russia in April 1917 to lead the Bolsheviks. Forced into hiding in July 1917, he re-emerged after the Bolshevik victory in October to become Chairman of the Council of People's Commissars, a post he held until his death.

Lvov, George E (1861–1925)

Head of the Zemstvo Union. he had done much to organise the war effort under the Tsar. Chosen as a liberal Prime Minister for the first Provisional Government by the leader of the Kadet Party, Milyukov, he was in fact more of a populist and urged a decentralised system of government in Russia. Replaced by Kerensky in July 1917.

Martov (Tsederbaum), Julius Ossipovich (1873–1923)

A close collaborator of Lenin until the 1903 split when he became the leader of the Menshevik faction. He took the same position on the First World War as Lenin and found himself as the leader of the Menshevik Internationalists. This group was prepared to work within the Soviets but it was further weakened by splits in 1918.

Milyukov, Paul Nikolayevich (1859–1943)

A professor of history, he founded the Constitutional Democratic Party (Kadets) in 1905. He was close to the British Ambassador and hoped for a Westminster-style constitutional monarchy. He became Foreign Minister (and the real force) in the first Provisional Government but was forced out over his views on continuing war until victory in 1917. Subsequently looked for a military dictatorship to save Russia from the Soviet system. He emigrated to Paris.

Rodzianko, M. V. (1859–1924)

An extremely wealthy landowner who joined the Octobrist party. He became Chairman of the Fourth Duma where he loyally tried to serve the Tsar and support Russia's war effort. He was the head of the Duma's Provisional Committee which set up the first Provisional Government. Went into exile in November 1917.

Shlyapnikov, Alexander (1883–1937)

Metalworkers' Union leader after 1917. An important Bolshevik organiser in the capital. After the revolution he became Commissar for Labour and from 1920 to 1922 was the co-leader of the Workers' Opposition with Alexandra Kollontai. Arrested during the Moscow trials.

Spiridonova, Maria Alexandrovna (1884–1941)

A leading Socialist-Revolutionary who became a member of the Left SRs when they split in November 1917. Subsequently admitted organising the murder of Mirbach in June 1918 which was the signal for the Left SR break with the Bolshevik system.

Stalin, (Djugashvili) Joseph Vissiaronovich (1879–1953)

Georgian origin. Joined the Social Democrats in 1898. Exiled to Siberia, returned in 1917 to take over the editorship of *Pravda*. Went into hiding after the July Days and spent much of the civil war organising resistance to the Whites around Tsaritsyn (which he later renamed after himself as Stalingrad). Tended always to take a middle course in debates ('a grey blur' according to Sukhanov). After the death of Sverdlov, he took on the role of General Secretary of the Party. Used this position so that by the end of the 1920s he had emerged as virtual dictator of Russia – a position he maintained until his death.

Sukhanov (Himmer), Nikolai Nikolayevich (1882–?)

Initially a non-party socialist who tried to reconcile Marxism and Populism, he eventually became a Menshevik-Internationalist close to Gorky and Martov. Wrote a rich chronicle of the events of 1917 but did not witness the final Bolshevik decision to prepare an insurrection. It took place in his own house from which his wife, the Bolshevik Galina Sukhanovna, had ensured his absence. After the October Revolution he took various posts in the government. Sent to a labour camp after the Show Trial of 1931.

Sverdlov, Yakov Mikhailovich (1885–1919)

A Social Democrat from the age of 16 he was imprisoned many times under Tsarism. His organisational talents were early recognised by Lenin and during 1917 he performed miracles of organisation of the growing Bolshevik Party with hardly any resources. His early death has often been seen as a great blow to the Communist Party.

Trotsky (Bronstein), Lev Davidovich (1879–1940)

Known as 'The Pen' for his brilliance as a writer, he did not join either the Bolsheviks or the Mensheviks after the 1903 split but maintained his own Inter-District group. It initially tried to re-unite the Social Democratic Party, but in 1917 Trotsky and Lenin increasingly found that they were travelling the same path and Trotsky's groups fused with the Bolsheviks in July 1917. Imprisoned after the July Days, he was released to become Chairman of the Petrograd Soviet. Main practical co-ordinator of the Bolsheviks in November 1917, negotiated the Treaty of Brest-Litovsk in 1918, and formed the Red Army in the Civil War. His arrogance made him unpopular amongst the other Bolshevik leaders who prevented him from succeeding Lenin in 1924. Expelled from the Party in 1927, expelled from the USSR in 1929, and murdered by a Stalinist agent in 1940 in Mexico City.

Tsereteli, Iraklion Georgevich (1882–1959)

A Menshevik leader who was on the Praesidium of the Petrograd Soviet after the February Revolution. Became Minister of Posts and Telegraphs in the second Provisional Government in May 1917, and after the July Days became Minister of the Interior. He returned to his native Georgia after the October Revolution to take part in the Menshevik Caucasian Republic. He went into exile with its fall in 1921, and died in New York.

Zinoviev (Radomyslsky), Gregory Yevseyevich (1883–1936)

Joined the Russian Social Democratic Labour Party in 1901 and sided with the Bolsheviks in the 1903 split. A collaborator of Lenin, he opposed the 7 November rising, with Kamenev. Subsequently became Chairman of the Petrograd Soviet, Chairman of the Politburo and first Chairman of the Comintern Executive Committee. Sided with Stalin against Trotsky until 1927, joining the latter in the United Opposition. Victim of the Show Trials.

Glossary

anarchism A political philosophy which denies the need for the State, regarding it as an oppressive body. Whilst the followers of Marx believed that the state would 'wither away' once classes ceased to exist, the anarchists believed the state could be abolished overnight. The various anarchist groups in Russia had different views as to what kind of collective society should then follow.

Black Hundreds Popular name for Monarchist organisation notorious for its pogroms against Jews, socialists and workers.

Bolsheviks The 'Majority' – the name given to Lenin's faction of the Social Democratic Party after the split in 1903.

bourgeoisie The owners of the means of production (i.e. factories, mines, etc.) in modern industrial society. Often equated (not strictly accurately) with the expression 'the middle class'.

Cheka All-Russian Extraordinary Commission for Combatting Counter-Revolution and Sabotage (the Bolshevik political police set up in December 1918 which subsequently became the GPU, the NKVD, and is today the KGB).

Duma The Russian Parliament 1906–17

Entente Russia's alliance with Britain and France. The USA joined this alliance in April 1917.

glasnost policy of 'openness', increased freedom of information and discussion allowed under Gorbachev 1985–90.

Kadets Members of the Constitutional Democratic Party, founded in 1905 by Milyukov. They were seeking the growth of parliamentary democracy through the Duma.

kulak 'fist' or tight-fisted farmer, a term for a rich peasant.

Marxist Followers of Karl Marx (1818–83). He argued that capitalism was not the final form of human society but only a stage in the history of human development. It would inevitably be overthrown by the working class (or proletariat).

Mensheviks The 'Minority' of the Social Democratic Party after the split with Lenin in 1903.

mir The traditional peasant commune, under Tsarism, run by elders.

NEP The New Economic Policy, the Soviet programme 1921–28, to restore the economy by allowing some private enterprise.

Octobrists Political group, consisting of mainly country gentry and businessmen, established in October 1905. They aimed to work within the Tsarist regime to implement the policies of the Tsar's October Manifesto.

Okhrana Tsarist secret police

pogrom An organised massacre.

Politburo Political Bureau of the Central Committee of the Russian Communist Party. Introduced after the revolution when the Party grew and the Central Committee became too large.

populism Russian revolutionary movement which dated from the 1860s. Populists believed that the mir, or peasant commune, could form the basis of a future decentralised Russian socialism. Turned to terrorism early in its development. The Socialist-Revolutionary party was its twentieth century heir.

proletariat The industrial working class.

putsch A sudden attempt to seize power.

Social Democrats (RSDLP) Marxists who formed the Russian Social Democratic Labour Party in 1898 to transform Russia into a Marxist Workers' State.

soviet A committee or council, since 1905 it has come to mean a workers' council elected originally on the basis of immediate recall.

Sovnarkom Council of People's Commissars (the Russian Cabinet after October 1917).

Socialist Revolutionaries (SRs) The Socialist Revolutionary Party was formed in 1901 by intellectuals who wanted to win political power for the peasant masses (see populism). The party was always loosely organised in a number of factions.

zemstvo Rural local government body (first set up in 1864).

Index